THE SUN FARMER

THE SUN FARMER

The Story of a Shocking Accident,
a Medical Miracle, and a
Family's Life-and-Death Decision

MICHAEL McCARTHY

Ivan R. Dee
Chicago 2007

THE SUN FARMER. Copyright © 2007 by Michael McCarthy. All rights
reserved, including the right to reproduce this book or portions thereof in any
form. For information, address: Ivan R. Dee, Publisher, 1332 North Halsted
Street, Chicago 60622. Manufactured in the United States of America and
printed on acid-free paper.

www.ivanrdee.com

Library of Congress Cataloging-in-Publication Data:
McCarthy, Michael, 1962–
    Sun farmer : the story of a shocking accident, a medical miracle, and a
family's life-and-death decision / Michael McCarthy.
    p. cm.
    Includes index.
    ISBN-13: 978-1-56663-700-8 (cloth : alk. paper)
    ISBN-10: 1-56663-700-7 (cloth : alk. paper)
    1. Fink, Ted—Health. 2. Burns and scalds—Patients—Biography. 3. Burns
and scalds—Patients—Family relationships. I. Title.
RD96.4.M39 2007
362.197'110092—dc22
[B]
                                                              2006100484

ad majorem Dei gloriam

PREFACE

IT BEGAN with the boots. In the fall of 2003 I had heard about an Illinois farmer so badly burned in his tractor that only his feet were spared damage. He had been wearing a new pair of work boots.

That was all I knew, and all I needed to. I was a newspaper reporter, and I had wanted to write a lengthy story profiling someone who was seeking to return to the work he or she loved after a debilitating accident.

The moment I heard about this farmer, I felt compelled to find him, to see his house and his farm, to find out everything I could about this tragedy. How had he survived such a thing? What was his life like now? What was it like to come back from the brink?

Ted and Rhoda Fink, I came to learn, were a naturally shy couple, soft-spoken and modest. They were not publicity seekers. I first heard about them from a social worker who helped disabled farmers in Illinois. On my behalf, he asked them if they would be willing to talk to a reporter who was interested in telling their story. They debated for two weeks. Then one day Rhoda called.

As I sat in my office at the *Wall Street Journal* in Chicago, Rhoda told me the details of that cold November afternoon four years earlier, and the shape Ted was in currently. When I hung up, I sat at my desk, speechless, and somehow changed. I had to meet them.

We planned to get together on a Tuesday the week before Thanksgiving in 2003. The night before, I lay awake nervous. I had seen pictures of burn victims before, and I knew the phrase "burned beyond recognition." I didn't know what to expect.

The Finks graciously invited me into their home, and, from that day forward, into their fields and their lives. We had lengthy conversations, and over the next fifteen months my notebooks filled up. After shucking corn in the kitchen with Rhoda one day, she decided to show me the couple's bathroom shower, a revealing personal stage where some of the hardship of their new life played out. Eventually she shared her diary, hundreds of pages long, with her raw feelings written the day the accident happened and chronicled for months afterward.

I spent a whole season with the Finks, planting corn and soybeans in the spring with their younger son, Chris, and riding months later in a combine harvesting the crops with Ted. It was during our combine and tractor rides together that Ted would reveal intimate thoughts, how at times he felt like a shadow of the man he once was.

After spending months with Ted and seeing his joys and limitations, I began to reflect on the fact that medical advances had allowed him to survive an accident that a few years earlier would surely have been fatal. I couldn't help noting that his accident in late November 1999 occurred at the dawn of a new century in which science was to quicken its march into our lives.

To explore Ted's story, I turned to an unusual cast, to whom I am especially grateful. Among them are Walter F. Rutkowski, executive director of the Carnegie Hero Fund Commission, and Kenneth Robertson, at the Illinois Natural History Survey, who has a deep knowledge of prairie America. Ioannis Yannas, a visionary scientist who invented an artificial skin that has helped thousands of people, led me around his laboratory at MIT and helped me keep my technical footing. Dr. Michael Schurr, Ted's chief burn surgeon at the University of Wisconsin's hospital in Madison, guided me through the burn unit as well as Ted's imposing medical case file.

The Fink family, including Ted's sister Judy, kindly endured my endless questions and hosted me for more than three years. During that time I also relied on the loving support of my own family—my wife, Marci, and our treasured children, Matthew, Sadie, Eastin, and Gabrielle.

I am grateful to Kevin Helliker, Bryan Gruley, and Carrie Dolan, the *Wall Street Journal* editors who handled the original feature story on the Finks.

I especially appreciate the foresight of my patient and eagle-eyed editor and publisher, Ivan Dee. After reading the newspaper story on the Finks, he wrote to me out of the blue, asking if I wanted to expand their tale into a book. By taking the time to look deeper, I found much to say about heroism, the clay we are made of (and under our feet), and a love story like no other.

M. M.

Chicago
February 2007

CONTENTS

"Souls are like athletes, that need opponents
worthy of them, if they are to be tried and extended
and pushed to the full use of their powers,
and rewarded according to their capacity."
—Thomas Merton

THE SUN FARMER

I

SCORCHED EARTH

✸ RHODA WAS SITTING in the living room, reading the day's mail and sipping iced tea, when she heard the explosion. She ran to the front door and saw a massive, curling fireball. Ted was in the flames, she felt certain. She called 911, frantically asking for help at the farm.

It was a chilly, windless Saturday afternoon, just before Thanksgiving in 1999. At their corn and soybean farm in northwestern Illinois, the Fink family had just completed a successful harvest. The fields were cleared and barren. It was easy for two neighboring farmers to see the giant ball of flame and feel the rumble a mile away. They raced over and snuffed the fire engulfing Ted by throwing dirt on him. He reignited. Using a pocketknife, the men cut and tore away his clothes, which were glowing like embers. Ted twisted on the ground, letting out a roar.

Paramedics and firemen came and carried the tall, heavy man from a field of smoking cornstalks. Rhoda heard someone yell, "He's alive."

She could not bring herself to run to the scene, to see her husband, so she watched the rescuers from a distance. Shivering and helpless, she saw the ambulance stir up gravel and dust as it raced away.

Inside of thirty minutes the rescue workers from the volunteer fire department met the helicopter several miles from the Fink farm. In a cornfield, with the blades whirling overhead, they loaded Ted onto the chopper and watched it depart for St. Anthony's Hospital in Rockford. Rhoda and her brother-in-law Don drove furiously to get there, but by the time they arrived the emergency room had already decided that Ted was too badly burned to be treated there. He needed to get to a sophisticated burn unit, fast. The nearest one was more than an hour's drive away, in Wisconsin.

Soon thereafter the helicopter touched down on the big white cross at the landing pad outside the University of Wisconsin hospital in Madison. Dr. Michael Schurr, chief of the burn unit, began examining Ted. Rhoda arrived. Having driven all afternoon to see her husband, and having just missed him at the hospital in Rockford, she was finally back with Ted.

Whenever a burn victim arrived at the UW hospital, doctors would examine the patient and then use two body outline charts, front and back, to blacken the burned areas. This allowed them to calculate the exact proportion of burned body surface, a critical measure in determining how to treat the victim. Doctors added up the percentages for the blackened parts. The head of an adult, for instance, represented 7 percent. Each hand, 2.5 percent. When 10 percent of an adult's body surface suffered third-degree burns, the deepest ones possible, it was generally considered a major burn.

When Dr. Schurr tallied up the portions of Ted that were burned, his total was 93 percent. Reviewing the chart sometime later, Dr. Schurr remarked, "Basically, all black."

Fearing for Ted's life, Rhoda listened while Dr. Schurr told her that her husband of twenty-five years was burned on nearly every inch of his body. Only his feet, protected by a new pair of steel-toed boots, had been completely spared. Not many years earlier, surgeons had calculated the odds of mortality in burn cases by adding the victim's age and the percentage of the body severely burned. For Ted that meant 45 years old plus a 93 percent burn—a probable mortality of 138 percent. Certain death.

But Dr. Schurr offered a glimmer of hope. He had had some success with a new synthetic skin that had just come on the market. The man-made skin was designed specifically for people with large, life-threatening burns.

As the doctor spoke, Rhoda pictured Ted, who towered over her at six-foot-two. He scaled eighty-foot ladders up grain silos in his soiled coveralls and muddy boots, welded beams, repaired tractors, and ran their farm almost single-handedly. He often came into the house with dust in his greying hair and thick prairie soil under his nails.

Using the artificial skin could be risky, said Dr. Schurr. Infection might set in. Sometimes the skin did not adhere well all over the body, in which case Ted's chances for survival would be slim. To endure the pain of skin grafting and other procedures, he would have to be sedated into a coma and kept under for several months, with the possibility he would never reawaken.

Even if he survived, he would never be the same, the doctor told her. There was no telling whether he would be left in a vegetative state, his mind permanently enfeebled. The doctor could not tell her how much her husband would ever be able to do again, whether he could use his hands, walk, talk, think.

Only his two feet appeared sound. At that point all Rhoda had seen of him was his head. It had ballooned monstrously, and his ears were nearly gone.

She could barely comprehend what had happened earlier that evening. Details came in fragments. Ted was working in his tractor. The blast. The firemen rushing in. The smoking cornstalks. His torn coveralls on the ground, smoldering. As best the rescuers and neighbors could put it together, Ted's tractor seemed to have backfired while he was near a leaking propane tank—and the sixteen-foot container, which resembled an oversized water heater, exploded in a giant ball of flame.

The doctor asked: What would her husband want? Rhoda was not sure. The couple had never discussed such a predicament. Dr. Schurr told her, "This is going to be long and hard, but I can try to save him." He wanted to know that her resolve would not waver, that she would not choose to withhold treatment later if Ted took a bad turn. The process would be so arduous for the victim, and so emotionally draining for the family and the nurses, that the doctor thought stopping partway through treatment would not be wise.

"We either try this, and give it a hero's try—or not," he told her.

There was little time for a second opinion. Rhoda could agree to pull her husband from life-support equipment then and there, or gamble that the synthetic skin would give them a chance to recapture, in some form, the life they had known.

She needed to decide quickly, so they could start the lifesaving surgery, or not.

She thought to herself: "We'll beat the system. We'll be that one-in-a-million shot." Then she paused and looked at the doctor. "Unless you tell me there's no hope," she said, "we'll keep plugging on."

That night Rhoda wrote in black cursive script on the stationery in her room at the Best Western hotel near the hospital: "Oh, God, my Teddy. My Teddy! I love you so much, from every part of my being—my life, my light, my helpmate, my rock. Things have taken a 90-degree turn and I must learn to be the stronger one. I pray to God that I can do this."

Having made the decision to proceed with the synthetic skin, Rhoda felt exhausted. The farm was more than ninety miles away, worlds away. She knew that Ted faced months in the hospital, and she did not want to leave his side. "I hate to leave Ted at the hospital all alone," she wrote, "but I need to shower and get some sleep. . . . I can't live at the U of Wisconsin hospital for the next year, but I won't leave Ted alone here either. What to do!?"

It would be several days before she would visit the field where the explosion had occurred. The soil was scorched, and Ted's wallet was there, its credit cards melted inside. Meanwhile the doctors had placed Ted in a drug-induced coma. That was to be his circumstance for a half-year or longer, leaving Rhoda to live alone with the consequences of her decision.

"Ted's condition is very grave," she wrote in her hotel room. "I have been in prayer since the accident. Must wait to see God's plan. I've put the situation in God's hands because it is so overwhelming. . . . I pray that if Ted survives he will be accepting of all the decisions made. . . . My Teddy will never look the same—but I hope he'll still be the same in his heart and soul. I hope he will be able to farm in some capacity."

Over the next few days Dr. Schurr began wrapping Ted's body in a cocoon of the costly synthetic skin, which went by the brand-name Integra. Ted's back, rear end, and thighs, his legs, belly, chest, and most of his torso—all were draped in $100,000 worth of Integra, a thin translucent film that looks like wet lasagna and is made of shark cartilage and collagen from cow tendons.

The surgeons first sliced away all of Ted's charred and dead skin, then began applying the sheets of artificial skin, some the size of a piece of 8½ x 11 notebook paper, fastening them with sutures and surgical staples. Larger sheets of Integra, the man-made hide, could be used only on relatively flat anatomy, including the back, abdomen, and chest. Thinner strips had to be cut for his legs, arms, and joints to prevent wrinkling. The artificial skin had to be fastened carefully to create an airtight seal with Ted's muscle or with lower layers of deep skin tissue. When the doctors had finished their patchwork, Ted looked like a ruddy old quilt.

As 1999 neared its end, Ted's new home became bed No. 5 at the University of Wisconsin burn unit. It was there that Ted Arthur Fink began a new chapter of his life, under skin with U.S. Patent No. 4,947,840.

2

VOWS

RHODA THOUGHT it was for the sex, plain and simple. Ted liked to say it was really for the tax benefit. Whatever combination of motives there may have been, Ted was intent on accelerating their wedding date, to tie the knot before the close of 1974. They had been planning their wedding for early 1975, on Valentine's Day in fact. Then one day in the fall, Ted approached his fiancée and demanded: "How soon can we get married?" And before she could answer, he did, saying: "As soon as we can, let's do it." They reset the date for just after Christmas, on Saturday, December 28, 1974.

This rush to the altar didn't come as a great surprise to Rhoda, given Ted's earlier romantic misstep—his clumsy handling of their engagement. A full week after Ted had asked her to marry him, and she agreed, Rhoda was at a gathering of Ted's relatives when she said she assumed they wanted to see the ring. She punched her fist forward, plunging it into their stunned faces. Ted, she came to discover with a warm flush, had neglected to tell anyone the news that he and Rhoda were engaged.

Ted had felt a bit intimidated by Rhoda Dumroese. She was a few months older than he and, by his reckoning, a "city girl." She lived in Freeport, a town of some 28,000 then. It was about forty minutes away from the Fink family farm in Lanark, in western Illinois, not far from the Mississippi River. Some Freeporters viewed themselves as more refined than their counterparts in smaller towns like Lanark. And, in truth, the water tower in Lanark is not nearly as impressive as the one in Freeport.

Rhoda's high school friend, Kimber Krueger, lived down the street in Freeport. She was dating Bernie Wehmeyer, a tree of a man standing six-foot-six, who was a high school friend of Ted's in Lanark. All four were recent graduates. One day Bernie said to Ted, "Kimber says she's got a friend."

It was nearly Christmas 1973 when the four went out for the first time. Rhoda was twenty, and Ted was a month shy of twenty. The foursome went to Monroe, a town just over the border in Wisconsin, where the drinking age was lower than the twenty-one limit in Illinois. First stop was a dance hall called the Green County House, and then another, the White Elephant. They talked and talked and played pool late into the night. After they dropped Rhoda off, Rhoda gave Ted her phone number, which he promptly forgot. The next day he drove to Freeport to get a phone book and look it up.

The next time she heard from him it was Christmas Day, and Rhoda was at her grandmother's house. Amid all the noise and commotion of the gathering, Rhoda could not figure out why Ted was calling her just then, and could not really hear him, making for an awkward conversation. He was not calling simply to wish her a happy holiday. Eventually, it became clear, he wanted to go out again. She did too. "When I first met Ted," Rhoda recalled, "I knew he was the one."

In Ted, Rhoda saw a hardworking, physically strong man. "I loved his mustache," she recalled. The couple enjoyed each other and worked well together. He would pick her up in his '71 blue Nova, and they would amuse themselves as Ted turned the steering wheel of the car and pushed the floor pedals while Rhoda worked the stick shift as they drove around together. "He'd just clutch, and I'd shift," she said. Because of her "religious upbringing," Ted confided many years later, he was not allowed in those early days to handle very much of Rhoda, except for placing his hand on her knee. So his gearshift hand was free to rest there, he recalled, if she worked the gears. That confession later surprised Rhoda; she thought they were just goofing around with the car.

As a son, grandson, great grandson, and great-great grandson of a farmer, Ted felt he had much to teach his city girlfriend about farming. He drove her out to the fields and gave her agricultural lessons, including one session on "corn sex." He explained how the tassels, the little tails atop the corn stalk, were male, and the silks, the threads below, female. And "tasseling" was one stage of the romantic tango between the two.

By day Rhoda was working as an x-ray technician. Her field, like much of medicine in the early 1970s, was about to be transformed radically by technology. At the time she worked with neither CT scans nor magnetic resonance imaging. In time both those electronic advances would allow doctors to peer into the internal anatomy of their patients as never before, without the need to cut them open. But Rhoda had been trained to operate x-ray machines, so she spent her day in a lead apron, taking black-and-white shots of skeletons and sliding the large floppy films into envelopes.

In the evening she and Ted socialized more and more steadily. Being a devout Christian, Rhoda appreciated that Ted lived cleanly. He did not smoke or drink, and no one in his family drank, either. Or hers. Ted was an ox—strong, with broad shoulders. And there was that bushy mustache she loved. Talking years later about what she found so attractive about him in those early days, Rhoda once blurted out, "He was a good kisser, and had a good ass."

Six months after they began dating, Ted and Rhoda were driving one afternoon in his Nova when he stopped and said to her, "There's something for you in the glove compartment."

"I opened it up," Rhoda recalled, "and there was a ring."

Pastor George Schrader officiated their wedding ceremony at Immanuel Lutheran Church in Freeport. It was the same church where Rhoda's parents had been married twenty-eight years earlier, and the same place where Rhoda herself had been christened. She had four bridesmaids, including Kimber, each dressed in the dark pink that was strangely popular in the 1970s. On the cover of the wedding invitation was a quotation from 1 Corinthians: "And now abideth faith, hope and love, all three; and the greatest of these is love."

Before family and friends, Ted vowed to stick by Rhoda in sickness and in health. No one in the church that day could have known, when Rhoda replied in kind, how heavy her vows would be.

The newlyweds departed Immanuel Lutheran, heads bent and blinking amid a shower of rice, for their reception at the YWCA in Freeport. Afterward Ted and Rhoda packed into the blue Nova for a honeymoon of two weeks in Florida. They visited Disneyland, Cypress Gardens, and Daytona Beach. They went on a bus tour of the rocketry sights at Cape Canaveral, which Ted particularly loved. But sickness interrupted the bliss when Ted fell ill with the stomach flu; he couldn't stop throwing up. The charm broken, the couple headed home a week early. Ted was sick the whole drive home, and Rhoda had to contend with the stick shift in the Nova and acquaint herself with its temperamental clutch. She was unaccustomed to a stick shift: her copper-colored AMC Gremlin was an automatic.

Once they settled into their farm life together, Ted worked long hours in the field. He spent his winters fixing machinery and ordering seeds for the following season. By the end of March or early April it was time to fertilize. April was planting month. In the fall he had only a four- to six-week period to harvest all the grain, haul it to buyers, or store it in silos. During these busy times, sixteen-hour days were not unusual. Winters were, more or less, down time. Within three years of the wedding, Rhoda was expecting. Peter, their firstborn, arrived in September 1978; Chris was born in October 1980. Both were baptized at Ted and Rhoda's church, the First Lutheran Church in Chadwick.

By the time the boys were toddlers, Ted was taking them along in the tractor when Rhoda was at work in the hospital. "Peter would sleep on a blanket in the tractor, and when he'd wake up, he'd ride in my lap," Ted recalled. When the boys were that age, Ted was intrigued with business entrepreneurs. He once went to see Sam Walton, the founder of a fast-growing retail chain called Wal-Mart Stores, speak at a store in Princeton, Illinois. Later he went to see Dave Thomas, the founder of the Wendy's hamburger chain, who was visiting one of his restaurants in Freeport. Ted introduced himself to both men, thanked them, and shook hands. "I was interested in the bumps they had along the way," he recalled. He did not expect these captains of industry to be so down-to-earth. "I liked that they were like everybody else," Ted said.

Carroll County, where Ted and Rhoda made their home, defines rural. It is virtually a single field that measures 468 square miles, carved up with two-lane roads. Houses pop into view every few minutes as one drives through, then the landscape reverts to flat fields, to the horizon. Driving is particularly maddening when the corn is eye-high. Everything looks the same: row after row after row after row of stalks. Any sense of time slips away. One can be lulled into a trance, lacking landmarks or the familiar visuals so convenient to a sense of location. On any given day in this leafy labyrinth, the fabled Minotaur might well pop out between cornrows. Between the fields are roads with telling names: Ideal, Pilgrim, Pioneer, Harvest, Fairhaven, Eagle Point, Pleasant Hill, Peace and Quiet, Scenic Bluff, Livingood. Carroll County has only one stoplight, in the town of Savanna, on the banks of the mighty Mississippi.

The county is two and a half hours by car west of Chicago and just east of Iowa. It runs right up to the Mississippi River to the west. Its terrain is not completely flat.

There are steep hills, sandy plains, and palisade. But mostly it is flat prairie—so flat that the town of Mt. Carroll is actually just a hill that soars above the otherwise pancake topography. With few trees, the ground is blanketed by sunshine from corner to corner of the county, and when the fields begin to sprout, they take on the appearance of five-o'clock shadow as far as the eye can see.

Within Carroll County are two towns the Fink farmers eventually migrated to: Chadwick, to the south, and Lanark, to the north. They are ten miles apart. Both were formed as railroad depots as the tracks began stretching out across the state in the early nineteenth century like splintered lightning.

Lanark is located in some of the richest farmland in the country. Before it was developed, it was essentially a vast wheat field dotted with maple trees. At one time Lanark called itself "Maple City." For a time in the twentieth century, Maple City butter was made in Lanark.

Rhoda adjusted well to Lanark and made Ted a nice home at the farm. Over time, big silos replaced animal pens as Ted, like many farmers in the area, switched from less profitable cattle to grain. Since moist corn and soybeans can spoil, the crops had to be dried before they were stored. That meant using powerful grain dryers, loud industrial ovens that fired at two hundred degrees or so. Their fuel came in tanks of highly flammable liquid propane.

Marriage was rosy for the Finks. The boys grew; the farm thrived. There were ups and downs, mostly ups. In the winter of 1994, though, Ted's father died at home of cancer. It was the day before Ted turned forty. Arnold Fink had survived two

27

wives: Ted's mother, June, and his second wife, Faith, whom he had married about a year and a half after June died. Ted had just three years with his mother, then a little over a year with his grandmother, Cora, and then he was raised mostly by his stepmother.

Motherless for a time, Ted grew up rough and stoic. He manhandled his toys. "Any toy or other treat Ted received, he would tear apart," recalled his cousin, Don Patton. "Ted was a tough kid." One day the two boys were riding tricycles on the porch together. Pedaling away in circles, they suddenly bonked heads as they rode too close together. "I, who was three years older, cried," recounted Don. "Ted just bit his lip while our parents iced down the welts on our foreheads." Ted, who recalled the event many years later, said, "It hurt too damn much to cry."

When he came home after school, Teddy, as he was known to classmates, would feed the family's cows and pigs. Years after graduating from high school, he liked to tell people he was in the top ten of his graduating class. After a pause, he would add that there were forty students in the whole class. Among them were no wildly successful entrepreneurs like the Wendy's burger chain founder. Undeniably the top luminary from Lanark High School was Don Buss, a graduate from the 1930s. He had invented a material for keeping fishworms alive. He not only formulated the slimy substance but established a factory to make the stuff, which made its way into fish tackle boxes the world over. According to one town history, Buss "reportedly made more than a million dollars."

To help care for young Ted immediately after his mother passed away in 1957, Grandma Cora would pick up her grandson each Monday and keep him with her down at the farm in Chadwick until the weekend, when he would return home to Lanark. While at grandma's farm he missed his dog, a mutt named Short. Back and forth from house to house, Ted would drag his little stocking cap with a raccoon tail on the end. "He wore it all the time, it was his favorite, and he was so cute in it," recalled his big sister Judy.

Ted was too young to ride with his father in the tractors, a frequent child-care practice then, so he spent many joyful days playing with his grandmother. The elderly lady with the curly grey hair and the little blond boy made soap together some days. They would mix lye, charcoal ashes, and lard. After boiling and churning it, they would leave it to harden. Then they would slice it into small blocks. It was a laborious process that took hours to create the rough bars that could scrape the toughest soil out of coveralls and arms and legs. Grandma Cora had an old Chrysler New Yorker, and while the older kids were in school or working in the fields, she and Ted would drive down the dirt roads together looking through the brush for bears.

Sometimes Cora would drive Ted to nearby limestone quarries, and he would look for fossils of fish and plants. The soil of Illinois, having been dug by glaciers eons ago, was rich with plant and sea life frozen in stone. The fossils maintained a record of the inhabitants of the heartland well before it became vast, open prairie. As Ted reached for the stones with his left hand, or otherwise showed an inclination to be left-handed, his grandmother reprimanded him, teaching him to favor his other hand. She figured a dominant right hand would be more useful later in life.

3

MADISON

ON Thanksgiving Day 1999, around 8:15 in the morning, Rhoda and her nineteen-year-old son Chris left the farm with frost on the grass and headed for Madison. There they visited with Ted briefly. He was all bandages—a mummy, with an unrecognizable face. He was hooked up to a breathing machine. Rhoda brought some pictures of the farm and taped them to her husband's headboard. The family had Thanksgiving dinner on plastic trays in the hospital cafeteria.

The capital of Wisconsin, Madison, is the second largest city in the state after Milwaukee, seventy-five miles to the east. It is largely a college and government town, with a vibrant cultural and political life. It is named for President James Madison, who died the summer it was founded in the early 1800s. On the city skyline it is impossible to miss the imposing state capitol, whose white granite dome is modeled after the U.S. capitol in Washington, D.C.

The University of Wisconsin dominates the downtown area, with some 41,000 students pedaling and milling about in a town of about 221,000 people. State Street links the campus and the capitol square. Madison, once nicknamed "Mad Town," has long been a hotbed for liberal and progressive ideologies. Born just outside Madison, "Fighting Bob" La Follette, a congressman whose run for president in 1924 legitimized the Progressive party in the United States, founded the publication now known as the *Progressive*. In the 1960s and 1970s thousands of "counterculture" students marched and rallied in opposition to the Vietnam War. In 1970 the army ROTC building on campus was set ablaze and a bomb was exploded in Sterling Hall, which contained an army research center. The smoke has cleared, but liberal sentiments throughout Madison and its local government remain.

Through the university hospital staff, Rhoda found a basement apartment near the hospital for a hundred dollars a week. It was basic: a bathroom, bed, microwave, and refrigerator cube. She retreated there often and confided in her diary. Sitting with Ted for hours on end grew harder since she could not see his face, which was wrapped in bandages.

The day after Thanksgiving, nearly a week after the accident, Rhoda sat at a conference table with Dr. Schurr, an eye doctor, a nurse, and a nurse supervisor to review her husband's progress. "Ted is stable but very critical with basically all third-degree burns," Rhoda wrote later that night. "Dr. Schurr said he will have to remain on the ventilator till all the grafting is done. Up to SIX months. That was a low blow. I had hoped he would be conscious by February. Talked about what could go wrong down the road: kidney failure, liver failure, pneumonia, sepsis, etc. He painted a pretty gloomy picture.

"Should we press on? Yes, for now. I guess we move forward till Dr. Schurr says there is no hope. That isn't today. See how things go overnight."

In the back of her mind, Rhoda recalled later, she felt she had the option at that time to remove him from life support if she felt that was positively the best course. But she decided to take a small step rather than contemplate an extended journey. "Went to the grocery store tonight. I guess I'm in for the long haul."

Nine years younger than Ted, Dr. Schurr initially pondered whether it was worth trying to put his patient back together again. Running a burn unit that handled about 250 new victims a year, the doctor had inevitably made some tough calls. Burn units are highly specialized, and there are only about 125 of them in the entire country. Madison's is respectable but not usually listed among the elite in burn centers nationally.

Dr. Schurr took into account that Ted worked with his hands. His treatment plans for burn patients ranked three priorities: "Save life, save function, save cosmesis," or physical appearance, he said. He had to estimate, given the complexity of burn trauma and recovery, how disabled Ted might be if he could pull him through. In the past, after carefully weighing the toll of flames on ability and appearance, Dr. Schurr had not recommended saving everyone rolled into the unit.

Prematurely grey in his early forties, he recalled one case. "I had a woman, twenty-seven, with a burn. A drunk driver hit her, and the gas tank exploded. Both her hands needed amputation. Her face had deep, horrible burns. I advocated doing nothing, and the mother [who disagreed with that recommendation] has hated me ever since.

"So we worked on her. She didn't survive."

Before he operated on Ted, who was unconscious, Dr. Schurr said he and Rhoda had to try to divine what her husband would have wanted. "If Ted had been sixty-five and wheelchair-bound with dementia, that might have been a different story," he said. The doctor himself had two daughters, then three and four. He learned that Ted had two sons, Peter and Chris, then twenty-one and nineteen.

"It gets deep and mushy, what makes you happy in life," Dr. Schurr recalled. "I would not want to miss my kids' growing up." Rhoda recalled thinking, "He was my husband. I wanted to save him."

The existence of Integra, and Ted's likely prognosis after numerous surgeries, convinced Dr. Schurr that technically Ted could be kept alive. "This was a little bit of a physician-playing-God thing: Is saving him doable or not doable? Obviously I thought it was."

What the flames had spared figured into the doctor's calculation that saving Ted was worth a try. "Though his face was terribly burned, it's not like he was missing a nose. He wasn't blind," the surgeon said, recalling some of his reasoning. "I didn't think his hands would have to be amputated."

On one of those points, the doctor and Rhoda would soon face miscalculation.

At 9:30 on the evening after Thanksgiving, Rhoda sat with her tan spiral-bound journal. On its cover was a stick figure surrounded by the words "Me: A Personal Journal." At the bottom of the cover it said, "Write It Down! Memories Are All That's Left. Live, Love, Laugh. . . .

"Still worried about the right/wrong decision. Am I doing the right thing? What Ted wants? How will Ted feel if we make it through all this? I will try not to worry about that

(Ted's head) right now. Will worry when he wakes up. The boys and I talked & decided we will press on until there is NO hope. God bless us—help us—keep us."

On Sunday Rhoda began to fill in the page at 7 p.m. At the bottom of the page, already printed there, it said, "The good old days are here & now." "The situation is still very grave and Ted looks awful. Face is covered with gauze soaked in some solution. I pray to God for guidance and hope I'm doing the right thing for Ted. This was one situation we never discussed. I refuse to surrender this ray of hope now. If the situation changes, then I'll see. Hope to get some sleep this PM!"

On Monday the doctor told her some of the Integra was not sticking—was not "taking," as doctors say—and would have to be replaced. "Must pray most of this sticks. Tired tonight—don't know if I should be discouraged or optimistic, I just pray & pray for a miracle," Rhoda wrote.

Twelve days after the accident, surgeons became concerned about Ted's hands. "The implications of Ted with no usable hands leaves me devastated," Rhoda wrote. "Almost more than I can comprehend. I question what I have done with these choices.

"Tonight for the first time I ask the why-us question. I can see no reason for this pain and mental suffering. Why has God allowed this to happen to Ted? WHY—WHY—WHY? This is more than I can bear."

In between writing out Christmas cards on a Thursday in early December, Rhoda turned to her diary. "Ted remains so stable that I get very optimistic and hopeful. I hate to get just too full of it. Recipe for a fall. I pray God doesn't bring us so far, as in weeks into it, and then have a disaster. That would be too cruel. Ted is strong and with all the prayers and support I know it will have a good outcome."

The next afternoon Rhoda and Dr. Schurr discussed Ted's condition. "75 percent of Integra did not stick to legs. . . . Talks to me about if I want to keep fighting. How now it will be longer, harder without Integra on legs. What would Ted want? WHAT WOULD Ted want? I don't know!!! Cry & cry & cry. . . . This is almost more than I can stand. A nightmare from which there is no waking up. . . . God, what a mess."

The next day she wrote: "Quality of life is a big issue. Won't be able to do work like before. I hope if he survives he'll just be happy to be alive and with the boys and me." Then she added, "I sit with Ted a lot."

Had she bothered to look back to the entry in her journal just days before Ted's accident, Rhoda would have found that she had filled in the blanks next to the prompting words "People/Things that brightened my day" in this way:

"Blessings: 1) great weather 2) good day at work 3) Ted & Chris safe and well 4) great family 5) Harvest is wonderful." Elsewhere she wrote that she was planning to sew a layette for a friend's baby and that she had picked up some fabric on the way home from work. She also noted that she planned to scrub the floors at home before going to work the next day.

On Sunday, December 12, Rhoda decorated the Christmas tree in the burn unit with Ted's sister Judy and her husband, Don. The holiday was approaching, and Rhoda offered to decorate. The nurses directed her to a box with the annual

Christmas tree and decorations. When Rhoda tried plugging in the string of old lights, she found them dead. She drove to a drugstore and bought new ones. She and Judy and Don strung garlands and lights around the tree, which they pieced together.

Later that week Rhoda began attending a burn support group at the hospital. It was a small gathering, a handful mostly of burn survivors, including a man in his forties who had been severely burned in a tent fire as a child. The blaze had taken the man's ears. The group discussed what was on their minds that week, and gave a practicum on how to deal with day-to-day issues of handicaps and disfigured features. Rhoda was not eager to attend the next session.

One Wednesday afternoon she got a shock. Ted began to mumble incoherently. "Sat with Ted, he started to talk, he was twitching around some—breathing against the vent— SCARED ME!

"It will be a real scary day when he wakes up."

A hospital social worker arrived one morning, a day when about an inch of snow had fallen in Madison, and found Rhoda making out the last of her Christmas cards. He came to talk about the bill. Some twenty-seven days into Ted's stay, it stood at $192,000. Rhoda, numb, had no idea where she would get the money to pay it.

"I want Ted off the ventilator so bad—for him to be awake & talking. But I don't want him in pain & aggravated & worrying about the farm & the money & the bill, etc. I'm eager and yet fearful of that day."

Ever the farm woman, Rhoda carefully monitored and chronicled weather conditions each day in her diary. On Wednesday, December 22, she noted an historic bright moon, in which the moon was closest to the earth while the earth was closest to the sun, making a full moon appear 14 percent brighter than earlier in the month, when it was at its farthest point. This was the direct result of the heavens aligning in a way they had not for 133 years. The last full moon of the millennium turned out to be a lunar spectacle.

Her diary entry that day captured her routine over many days: "Sat with Ted, slept, read a book, went for a walk, came back, sat with Ted till 5:45 p.m."

The next night she wrote, "I'm still just terribly worried over Ted's hands. I just hope and pray that we can save the left one and have some fingers on the right. I just don't know how Ted will react if they can't save his hand/hands. I'll just keep praying for miracle #2. I also hope he will be happy to be alive and adjust to all the other (unknowns) problems he will face."

The diary entry for December 25: "Had 'Christmas' at Mom's this morning." The family opened presents and had green beans and potatoes and rolls and cookies.

The next Tuesday, December 28, was Ted and Rhoda's twenty-fifth wedding anniversary. Deb, the burn unit's secretary, baked a cake and brought in plates and napkins. Back at the farm, neighbors sympathized with Chris's plight, a teenage boy with neither parent around for days on end, and brought him food. The parade of meals on wheels stretched into months. "I didn't know there were so many ways to make chili," recalled Judy.

On the morning of New Year's Eve at the farm, Chris and Rhoda had a heart-to-heart. "We hash and rehash the same old stuff—are we doing the right things? What will Ted think, etc." She left for Madison around noon. When she arrived in Ted's room—"Surprise, his face is swollen! Yikes, it looks bad." She talked it over with a nurse who eventually settled her down. "Ted is OK! Stay calm, Rhoda," she later wrote.

In the hospital Rhoda began hearing anxious discussions about New Year's Eve. The world was approaching the new millennium with trepidation. Society had embraced the computer, but programmers implausibly had neglected to code them to recognize the rollover from 1999 to 2000, in what looked like a looming disaster being called Y2K. Dire forecasts made scare fodder for the media—planes falling from the air as flight-navigation systems went haywire; computer-locked prison doors suddenly opening; hospital power being zapped. There was no end to the doomsday scenarios.

In Madison the police department planned to beef up its ranks—almost a hundred officers out in force, nearly double the deployment for a routine New Year's. Anticipating the Y2K meltdown, the sheriff's office placed on duty its bomb-sniffing dog, the only one in the western part of Wisconsin. The *Madison Capital-Times* assured readers that the jail had emergency generators to keep the inmates behind bars. Law enforcement had contingency plans for all kinds of potential mishaps, from apocalyptic computer failures to traffic bottlenecks to terrorist attacks. Emergency management officials were squirreled away in a response center in the Public Safety Building. Tactical SWAT teams were poised at some of the police department's Y2K command posts around the city.

Emergency officials in Madison kept an eye on how midnight passed in Japan and New Zealand, and were relieved to see no reports of malfunctioning water, gas, or electrical power systems in those countries.

To Rhoda's relief there were no mishaps at the hospital, and little happened elsewhere as the old century passed away shortly after the Millennium Booms fireworks show in town. A five-pound, eight-ounce boy, the son of Andy and Karen Derrick of Beaver Dam, Wisconsin, was born at 12:48 a.m.— the first baby born at a Madison hospital in the New Year.

Ted slept through the millennial milestone.

On January 4 Rhoda took down the burn unit's Christmas tree and packed it away with the decorations. On a Friday, with snow flurries outside, she wrote, "My state of mind is better today, but I still worry about the final outcome. . . . I hope he doesn't hate me. . . ." A little later she wrote, "New skin looks great. I'm holding my breath it will take. Hard to visit when I don't see his face. I thought his ears were in better shape, but I don't think much is left."

With Ted in a coma going on two months, Rhoda had two constant companions: her diary and his wedding ring, which she began wearing on a necklace. Ted did not usually wear it because it could be a hazard around the machinery he worked with on the farm. He kept it in the "junk box" on their bedroom dresser. After the accident, Rhoda went back to the house, dug it out of the box, and slid it onto the chain.

On a cold and sunny Thursday late that January, Rhoda's stomach suddenly turned while she was at the grocery store. She was standing in line to check out when she noticed she did not have Ted's wedding ring. It was gone. She hunted and retraced her steps, scanning along the floor aisle by aisle. Coming up empty, she alerted the store manager, who promised her he would notify her if it turned up.

"I'm just sick, sick, sick. I KNEW I shouldn't be wearing it, and was taking a chance with it," she confided to her diary later that night. "I'm so upset and angry with myself. I went back and looked and looked, but it was an exercise in futility. UW hospital is a big place.

"I don't know what I'll tell Ted. Damn—I'm just so angry with myself over this. I just wanted to feel closer to him. Crap."

Trying to absorb that loss, Rhoda soon became apprehensive about another. When Chris showed up at the hospital the following Sunday, "We talked over all the farm stuff," Rhoda wrote. "It makes my head swim. I have a hard time switching between hospital mode and farm mode. I pray it all works out. I don't want to lose the farm to the hospital, but I really don't want to lose it because we screwed up. Must be tired tonight—it's almost too much to bear." Bills in the burn unit were running about five thousand dollars a day. The Finks' private insurance was exhausted.

Later in the week it was Ted's forty-sixth birthday. Rhoda made brownies and cookies for the nurses and got some blond highlights in her hair. The nurses sang "Happy Birthday" to Ted, though he was comatose, and toasted him with sparkling grape juice. And Rhoda herself had received a gift. The manager from Sentry Foods called. A grocery store clerk had found Ted's ring while sweeping the floor.

As the first month of 2000 drew to a close, things were looking up. But doctors were concerned about the stubborn refusal of Ted's right hand to heal, particularly his thumb. With the loss of a thumb the whole hand loses nearly half its function. The thumb is critical to so many simple daily tasks, like holding a pen or a fork or turning a doorknob, that surgeons sometimes transplant a finger or even a toe, in a rather bizarre operation, into the thumb's spot just to restore gripping ability. "Without the thumb," the anthropologist-physician John Napier wrote in the early 1980s, "the hand is put back 60 million years in evolutionary terms."

On the last day of January 2000, Ted's right thumb was amputated. Rhoda wrote, "I dream about Ted a lot. I miss talking and interacting with him very much. I can't wait for the day they wake him up and he's coherent."

Then she added, "His right hand looks sad without the thumb."

By Rhoda's own accounting, her husband looked awful that February. "Still red and sore looking, bleeds. The grafted skin is so very thin and fragile. His body is still swollen with extra fluids around the face, feet, fingers." Rhoda had a talk with Dr. Schurr about waking Ted up. She told her diary, "Pretty scary to me."

By mid-February she was convinced he would pull through, and concerned about what he was going to make of what he had become. As Rhoda wrote many times in variations of these words, "I'm getting nervous about the big wake up."

For the next few months she stared at the barren branches on a honey locust tree outside room No. 5 at the burn unit. She daydreamed about how life had been.

4

MIT

W HUMAN SKIN is nature's miracle blanket. The average adult has twenty-one square feet of it, weighing about seven pounds and comprised of about 300 million skin cells. The epidermis, the thin surface layer visible to the outside world, is only about a millimeter, or four-hundredths of an inch, thick, roughly the same as seven pieces of paper pinched between your fingers. It is thicker on the palms and the soles of the feet, both areas that need tough coverage, and much thinner on the eyelids, which need rapid movement for effective eye protection, and for flirting. The skin helps regulate the body's temperature, sweating or shivering to keep it at an optimal 98.6 degrees. It is a pliable fortress, shielding the body's inner anatomy from bacterial assaults.

Reinforcement is constant. New cells, formed by division at the very bottom of the epidermis, begin a climb that lasts anywhere from one to three months. These epidermal cells are alpinists, ascending constantly. The process is critical because the body routinely sheds some thirty thousand to forty thousand dead cells from the skin's surface every minute.

Virtually waterproof, human skin is a thicket of subterranean anatomical roots, including arteries, veins, and capillaries. It contains pigment cells that determine someone's color. On average, each squared half-inch of skin, that is, one this size,

contains 10 hairs, 15 oil (or sebaceous) glands, 100 sweat glands, and 3.2 feet of winding blood vessels. It is a marvelous and intricate network, durable enough to withstand the everyday friction of the world's hustle and bustle, yet delicate enough to feel tickly when a fly prowls around.

Saving this precious organ has long confounded surgeons. For centuries victims of fires often could survive the flames, but having lost the precious protection of their skin they soon succumbed to bacterial infection. Until the early 1940s the commonly accepted practice for treating badly burned people was to slather dyes and tannic acid on their damaged skin. The hope was that by covering the burned areas, infection could be sealed out. The problem was that infection often welled up from the burned skin underneath the topical treatments.

In 1942 surgeons at Massachusetts General Hospital decided to try an experimental approach to this problem, after a fire at the Cocoanut Grove nightclub in Boston. After the blaze broke out one grim Saturday night, emergency rooms around town were overwhelmed, and 492 of the nearly 1,000 people at the club that night perished.

At Mass General, surgeons deviated from standard practice and immediately began cutting out the badly burned skin of victims and covering the exposed areas with grafts, or large pieces of unburned skin. They were able to cut the rate of infection dramatically and improve the patients' chances for survival—but only for a time.

By quickly cutting away the burned skin, the doctors had helped more people survive in the initial hours and days after the fire. Before that, perhaps mercifully, victims who lost much of their skin to fire often didn't last even that long. The surgical advance in Boston, however, created an altogether new problem. Victims were being saved as never before, but they lacked enough of their own healthy skin to cover up the damaged areas. Infection was creeping in and again claiming victims. Death had only been postponed.

The problem for survivors was that while their upper layer of skin, the epidermis, regenerated, their lower portion, the dermis, physically did not. So victims who lost large parts of their dermis, in deep burns, required implanted skin. Again, when patients lacked enough of their own skin to donate as covering for their burned spots, surgeons had to find some alternative, and they often employed dressings of pigskin or skin from human cadavers as a substitute. These worked temporarily, but only as a Band-Aid. The body's immune system often turns on these kinds of grafts, mistaking them for dangerous invaders. So an individual's own skin is the only long-term solution.

By the late 1960s a surgeon named John Burke, who was chief of staff at the Shriners Hospital in Boston, was fed up with losing patients in this manner to infection. The only solution, he had determined, was to begin development on some sort of synthetic skin, a lifesaving product that could be stocked in burn units, at the ready for emergencies. "The decision to jump into the adventure of developing an artificial skin occurred when it became absolutely clear to us that in big burns there wasn't enough patient skin to close the wounds," said Dr. Burke. "To solve the problem, we had to develop something that was manufactured. It was the only possible solution for saving people's lives."

Fabricating skin, in all its complexity, proved frustrating. Trying to devise the world's first artificial skin, Dr. Burke worked with a chemist and others for more than a year, experimenting with a variety of compounds. For the most part they were concocting what Dr. Burke came to refer to as "glorious messes." They weren't even close. The concept of synthesizing skin seemed impossible.

In late 1969 the discouraged Dr. Burke received a phone call from a Greek immigrant who was to change the history of burn care and artificial skin. Ioannis Yannas had had an intense scientific curiosity from the time he was a teenager in Athens, Greece, in the 1940s. That was when he read the *Microbe Hunters*, the classic best-seller by Paul de Kruif, a bacteriologist and pathologist. The book dramatizes the breakthrough bacteriological research of such technical giants as Antonie van Leeuwenhoek, the first man to use a microscope to observe bacteria and protozoa; Joseph Lister, who pioneered antisepsis in surgery; and Louis Pasteur, whose laboratory work developed a new sterilization process that made food safer and who discovered cures for rabies and other diseases. Of all of them, Pasteur particularly impressed young

Yannas. Pasteur was a chemist who gained world renown by going into medicine.

Gifted in mathematics as a youth, Yannas decided to leave Greece to pursue his education as a scientist in America. He applied to Harvard University to study chemistry. It was the mid-1950s, and his father, a successful textile merchant in Athens, could tell where the future lay. His suggestion to his son could have come straight out of the famous scene from *The Graduate*, the countercultural coming-of-age movie in which Dustin Hoffman, fresh out of college, is accosted by a family friend who looks him in the eye and offers him one word of advice for his future: plastics.

On that path, Yanni Yannas studied chemistry at Harvard and through the early 1960s worked as a research chemist at the Grace Chemical Company in Cambridge. A physical chemist by training, Yannas had not gone to medical school. But the call of medicine and the ghost of Pasteur kept haunting him. While at Princeton, studying for his doctoral degree, he began working with polymers, or synthetic compounds such as nylon. Polymers can also be made from natural materials such as collagen, a fibrous protein found in bones, skin, and cartilage. That was the type of polymer that intrigued Yannas. "I was trying to figure out how to enter the field of life sciences from the avenue of physics," he explained in his thick Greek accent. Eventually that led him to the labs of the vaunted Massachusetts Institute of Technology.

Through his contacts at nearby Massachusetts General, Yannas heard about the ill-fated attempts to develop an artificial skin. He had a hunch this might be the avenue between physics and life sciences he had been hunting for. When he talked with Dr. Burke, the two men agreed to propose a project, an artificial skin, for funding from the National Institutes of Health, the federal agency that finances much of the biomedical research in the United States. Around this time, in the late 1960s, the world's first heart transplant had been conducted, and, emboldened by this dramatic development, the National Institutes of Health and other research groups were eager to push the frontiers of organ replacement. A synthetic skin, which could help soldiers burned and maimed on the battlefield, was one such promising organ substitute.

As part of their work together, Yannas arranged to accompany Dr. Burke on rounds at Shriners Hospital, checking on severely burned patients. Dr. Burke showed Yannas patient after patient, explaining that he desperately needed something to make wounds close faster, something that lasted longer than cadaver skin.

"I was so struck by seeing these people, deformed," recalled Yannas. "It hit me very deeply."

Visiting Yannas at his lab at MIT, Dr. Burke arrived at the massive main Rogers Building on Massachusetts Avenue, not far from the Charles River. With its colossal stone pillars, the edifice resembles the U.S. Supreme Court building. There Dr. Burke stepped through a double door into Yannas's lab. Written in blocky capital letters on the dingy cream-colored glass of the left door it said, POLYMER PHYSICS LAB, and on the right door, CHARLES T. MAIN TEXTILE RESEARCH LABORATORY.

The brainy, mathematical nature of MIT is evident in its campus numbering system: a single room number identifies the precise location of every room in the complex of buildings. Yannas's lab was 3-315. Under the code, the first numeral represents the building number. After the hyphen is the floor number, the third floor, and then the specific room, 15. Yannas's own office, with shelf after shelf stuffed with research reports and textbooks, was 3-332. The men's room across the hall was 3-331.

Working with glass Petri dishes in his white lab coat, Yannas and his students developed a number of recipes for a flimsy, polymer-based sponge, about as thick as a paper towel. After trying different forms of collagen, the protein that is a main building block of human skin, Yannas settled upon a concoction that was a blend of shark cartilage and cow tendons. He freeze-dried it in a carefully controlled, multi-step process to create tiny holes in it and thus make it highly porous. The meshlike nature of the artificial skin, with those little tiny cavities, became a huge part of the success of the invention, as the polymer chemist and the burn surgeon would later come to discover.

Early tests were made on the proverbial guinea pig. It was 1974, and Yannas, with technicians at the Shriners Hospital, toiled over the little animals, grafting the artificial skin under their pigskin or onto their open wounds. In mammals, one of the key wound-healing mechanisms is called contraction, in which the skin literally tightens up and closes around a hole in it. Nature, it seems, has a built-in means for closure—the very term used by psychologists to describe what patients with emotional traumas need.

Word of what was brewing in the MIT labs leaked out just after Christmas in 1975, and the NBC affiliate Channel 7 in Boston opened a broadcast with this report: "A breakthrough has been made in the development of artificial skin."

Switching to the lab, the broadcast showed Yannas in his crisp lab coat and thick black glasses, wearing rubber gloves, bending and manipulating a round white piece of artificial skin. He then was shown peering into a microscope. "What Yannas sees in his microscope," the reporter began, "are magnifications of various polymer compounds grown from animals. These collagen fibers, when properly mixed, most resemble human skin.

"Although still in the experimental stage, its development could mean renewed hopes for the victims of massive fires that take the lives of ten thousand Americans in home fires alone every year." The next night Channel 5, the ABC affiliate, followed that report with its own visit to the polymer lab.

In the glow of the media spotlight, Yannas and his team at MIT were now under pressure to produce. Early results were exciting but confusing. Even though the ingredients of their product came from other animals, a particular combination of collagen from cow tendons and the sugarlike molecule glycosaminoglycan from shark cartilage was not rejected by the guinea pigs. Not only that, the porous sheet became stuck onto the tissues of the animals by what looked like new, thick tissue.

In these early tests the artificial skin prototype also had a surprising and disconcerting side effect. While it was covering open wounds effectively and reducing the likelihood of infection, it was also slowing the rate of contraction: the body's conventional route to healing was being retarded. Any delay of skin contraction was not what surgeons like Dr. Burke wanted.

"I felt like a failure," recalled Yannas, eminently fearful that he might be out of his element in designing replacement body parts without a medical degree. "I thought, 'Here I am, a chemist—I don't know what I'm doing." The artificial skin project seemed to have hit a wall.

"Then it came to me," said Yannas. "If we had a pretty secure way of doing it wrong, we could find a way to do it right." Over time and repeated reformulations, the scientists perfected a recipe for artificial skin that in many ways mimicked the dermis.

As it turned out, Yannas did apply his father's advice about plastic. To replicate the epidermis, he developed a 1/10 millimeter-thick layer of the artificial skin using a Dow Corning material called Silastic, a plastic based on the chemical element silicon. Silicon is a brittle element that is abundant the world over, found naturally in beach sand and granite, and used in semiconductors and concrete. Following chemical reaction with several other elements, it is also used in silicone breast implants. In burn treatment, after the artificial dermal layer has broken down and the new dermis is formed, surgeons can peel off the plastic layer on top, replacing it with grafts—the thin portions of unburned healthy skin from elsewhere on the patient's body. Yannas and Dr. Burke found that their twin-ply artificial skin recreated the protective seal of the skin, keeping tissue and organ fluids inside the body while locking out harmful bacteria.

Yannas had an inkling of insight into the contents of his stainless steel lab trays one day in 1975, when an African-American TV reporter, Jim Boyd, spoke with the scientist off camera. The reporter looked at the white foamy material that was purported to be a breakthrough and said to Yannas: "This is going to be useful to many people, but what about somebody like me with black skin?" A reasonable question, Yannas thought, looking at the light color of the artificial skin. As he paused to formulate his response, a light bulb went on. He began to see that he was making not simply a wrap or a covering of replacement skin but a little seedbed for the body's own nerves and collagen to creep back into. And along with the returning cells that were unique to the patient would be the pigment cells that determine the coloration of skin.

Yannas and his colleagues discovered that they had created a biologically active "matrix" that effectively coaxed the skin dermis to regenerate, something it did not do naturally. That put Yannas on a quest to perfect the artificial skin not only to help people restore skin they had lost but also to see if the matrix technology could be replicated to induce other organs in the body to regenerate. Perhaps a different template could help veins repair themselves, and still another, kidneys. All theoretical, at that point, but an intriguing possibility.

By the late 1970s Yannas and Dr. Burke believed they were ready to begin clinical trials on the artificial skin. Yannas prepared supplies in the lab, and arrangements were made to treat newly burned patients who arrived at Shriners Hospital and at Massachusetts General. An initial group of ten burn victims would be tested. The unfortunates, aged three to sixty, arrived at the hospitals in critical condition with burns over 50 to 90 percent of their bodies. They were told about the experimental skin, its benefits and risks, and gave their informed consent.

Shortly after the trial, Dr. Burke appeared in Chicago— not ninety miles from the Finks' farm—to report on this research at the annual meeting of the American Surgical Association. It was chilly, late April 1981. In earlier papers Dr. Burke had laid out the dire need for an artificial skin. Roughly 1.5 million Americans were being burned each year. Some 75,000 of them required hospitalization, and 5,000 to 12,000 died annually of their burn injuries. Most patients with burns over 60 percent or more of their body died: there was simply no way to heal them with their own skin grafts alone.

Before the surgeons in Chicago, Dr. Burke explained how the artificial skin was being produced at MIT. The collagen was being derived from cowhide donated by the Department of Agriculture's Philadelphia office. Researchers cut the hides into strips, then heated and cooled them in precise steps to extract the collagen, which was then freeze-dried at two different points to create a spongy, pliable mesh. Once the artificial skin was ready—it looked a bit like the softener sheets one throws into a clothes dryer—it could be stored at room temperature. It was capable of large-scale production, Dr. Burke told his colleagues.

He gave them a glowing report of the clinical trial, acknowledging that it had been tried on only ten people, scarcely a large enough sample to be conclusive. But it was an encouraging start. All ten patients had been burned with flames; seven were male. Their body surface area had been treated with 15 to 60 percent coverage of artificial skin. In all cases, within fourteen to forty-six days, the outer plastic layer, the Silastic, was removed and successfully replaced with thin skin grafts from the patients themselves.

Standing before a skeptical and expert body of his peers, Dr. Burke had to concede this: "There is, of course, no evidence indicating that the anatomic arrangement with its functional and cosmetic benefits will persist for long periods of time." But he also explained how the research team was surprised to find that when this two-ply layer of skin was laid over burn wounds, it acted like a scaffold. The tiny holes seemed to entice nerves and veins to snake their way through the dermal layer, bringing feeling back to the surface of the patient's skin. It was an unexpected bonus; trying to reengineer sweat glands and hair follicles back into the artificial skin would have been too complex. Yannas and Dr. Burke, it appeared, had a real breakthrough on their hands.

Having delivered his report, Dr. Burke faced the gauntlet of peer review. Doctors nationwide had had their doubts about the viability of this artificial skin, and they now had their chance to confront its developer face to face. "Dr. Burke and I have argued about this from time to time," began Dr. Thomas K. Hunt of San Francisco. Dr. Hunt had wondered whether the artificial skin actually did grow new veins. "I asked him for a small sample of it," Dr. Hunt told the group. "We put a couple of slivers into the cornea of some rabbits' eyes." The audience looked at him, then at Dr. Burke. Dr. Hunt continued, "And then we sat down and watched it become neovascular under the slip lamp. It was quite a magnificent thing to watch."

Dr. Hunt added that Dr. Burke's work helped "show how a healing wound can be directed to do the bidding of the surgeon. I hope this will put an end to a long-held feeling that wound healing is an unmalleable process, and show once and for all that we can influence it to do our own work for us." A few other skeptics were similarly converted.

To this glow of praise Dr. Burke responded, "I think it is important to recognize that the simple wound-dressing days have ended and that the wound manipulation days have begun." Then, in a seeming nod to his own accomplishments and to his anticipated laurels, Dr. Burke cited an acclaimed

French surgeon. "Ambroise Paré's concept, giving the dressing to us and the healing to the Almighty, may no longer be completely accurate," Dr. Burke said. The French physician, often called the father of modern surgery, was one of the most highly regarded surgeons of the European Renaissance, having served four monarchs: Henry II, Francis II, Charles IX, and Henry III. In his long career, which stretched from the early 1530s until almost the end of the century and involved much battlefield surgery, Dr. Paré introduced implanted teeth and artificial limbs as well as gold and silver artificial eyes.

Looking forward, Dr. Burke concluded: "We are now in a phase in which we are going to be able to manipulate the character, the speed and the quality of healing to some extent, so that we can achieve healing that has not been possible and with a quality that has not been possible in the past."

If his words seemed boastful, within two years they gained a ring of truth. In 1983 Ino Papageorgiou, an architect who lived in Newton, Massachusetts, was suddenly hurtled through the closed door of her kitchen following a violent explosion. The fifty-year-old woman, originally from Greece like Yanni Yannas, had been cleaning the floor with a powerful solvent. The doors and windows were closed. When the gathering fumes were apparently ignited by a pilot light in the stove, she was burned over 80 percent of her body.

At the time of this accident the MIT lab could manufacture only about ten square feet of skin over a few days, roughly the amount needed for someone who was burned over 50 percent of the skin surface area. Upon hearing of the woman's accident, a friend, Daphne Hartsopoulos, who was familiar with the research in Yannas's lab and his collaboration with Dr. Burke, called Yannas within hours to ask if something could be done to save Ino's life.

Yannas and his students and co-workers began operating the MIT lab twenty-four hours a day to manufacture the artificial skin for Ino. Still in testing, it was not yet available on the market. The pieces of artificial skin were carefully transported from MIT to Massachusetts General where Dr. Burke was now chief of trauma services. Ino was treated over almost her entire body with the membrane, and within weeks began growing her own skin. She survived multiple surgical procedures and later returned to her native Greece.

About three years later, in 1986, Ino saw Yannas and his daughter Tania, thirteen, and son Alexi, nine, strolling in downtown Athens, where they were vacationing. As Yannas recalled it, "She approached us, took my hands in hers, and said to my children: 'Your father saved my life.' For me, this was probably the high point of my life."

The MIT researchers had initially designed the spongy artificial skin with pores that were smaller than those normally found in skin. They quickly found out, however, that such tiny bubbles prevented some of the body's cells from migrating into the artificial-skin template. After enlarging these pores to a size that turned out to be a critical component of the skin's biological activity, they found that the artificial skin tricked the body and acted like a snake charmer, luring winding nerves to grow up into the bottom layer, the artificial dermis. That restored feeling for patients.

By the early 1980s it became clear that the MIT team had turned human biology upside down. Their discovery was the first demonstration of inducing an organ that didn't normally regenerate to do so. The surprising reversal of human anatomical nature led to Yannas's being elected to the Institute of Medicine of the prestigious National Academy of Sciences.

The discovery showed Yannas that for some time he had been on the wrong path with his work. In the early days he had tried to synthesize in the lab a novel fiber-reinforced material based on proteins found in nature, mechanically as strong as normal skin—in short, a bioengineered skin that would be as tough and as pliable as the skin that nature itself provides us. In his office Yannas kept the nose of a NASA rocket, a sturdy cone made from then state-of-the-art reinforced composite materials. He was trying to do roughly the same thing with skin. The original idea was to replace the burned dermal layer with an artificial one that would be as mechanically competent as normal skin and would remain in place permanently.

But as the MIT group worked along this path, it became clear after a few trials that it was preferable for the graft to act as a temporary scaffold. It would stay in place only while the body itself reconstructed the dermal layer. The concept of a skin replacement that, once grafted, would remain in place unchanged, permanently replacing skin, was set aside. Yannas was astonished at what he and his team had accomplished. "Our materials were instructing the tissue to make something other than a scar," he said.

This finding foreshadowed the dawning of a field called regenerative medicine. People in dire need of a replacement kidney or pancreas or heart face a constant shortage of donated organs. What if surgeons could implant a scaffold that, similar to the dermal layer of skin, could prompt a kidney to regenerate healthy kidney tissue? It is not as farfetched as it may sound. It is the same sort of quest that stem-cell researchers have been on. In their case, they have been trying to harvest embryonic stem cells that will instruct the body in its early stages to grow this or that organ.

Yannas wondered if his bioactive scaffolds were somehow awakening the innate ability for regeneration that is characteristic of early human fetuses. He kept turning over TV reporter Boyd's question in his head. "It prompted me to think, for the first time that day, that it might—just might— be possible that a black person could get his own black skin back. This was the first time I thought of the possibility of re generation, that the artificial skin was conceivably inducing regeneration in the long run, rather than a wound dressing with certain desirable short-term properties.

"The possibility of regeneration had not occurred to any of us working in the field at that time. I had difficulty publishing the term 'regeneration' because it appeared to be somewhat absurd." So as Yannas edged toward disclosing his discovery, the titles of his papers were initially clunky and cautious. There was a 1981 paper titled "Prompt, Long-term Functional Replacement of Skin." And the next year, "Wound Tissue Can Utilize a Polymeric Template to Synthesize a Functional Extension of Skin." To avoid being viewed as a nut or laughed out of the scientific community, he purposely avoided the term "regeneration."

This all raises one of the human body's great evolutionary mysteries. Why do some animals regenerate but people don't? High school biology textbooks routinely show photos or drawings of the spectacular feat of regeneration of some flatworm species. Cut in two, each piece will regenerate an entire body. After a limb is amputated on many newts, salamanders, and tadpoles, almost perfect replacement limbs sprout. When male deer shed antlers in the spring, they inevitably grow new ones.

People are not as talented. Early in their anatomical development, typically in the first six months in the uterus, mammalian fetuses can actually heal their wounds by regeneration. But sometime in the last trimester that ability is lost, and from then forward, wounds are healed in the human being in two ways: contraction, or a shrinking of the wound, and scarring. Scientists do not know why this change has evolved. Regeneration would seem to be a superior ability, so why would evolution not have passed along the gift of regrowth? Some researchers have theorized that in the womb the baby does not need wound healing since it is wholly enclosed in the protective environment of the mother's body. Later, though, as the early mammals, and later the early hominids, were jumping from branch to branch, if one were to tear his skin or were bitten by a predator, he could die from infection—without a mechanism for fast healing. Scars and contraction amount to nature's bandages. Human evolution may have decided it was a waste to expend the enormous amount of precious energy needed to regrow an arm or a leg when shrinking of the wound together with formation of a simple scar did the trick nicely.

Fibrosis, or healing through scars, is by far the most widespread means that mammals use to repair injuries. One exception in humans is the liver. For reasons that are unknown, that organ does regenerate to original mass, or size, but not in its original shape. If 70 percent of the organ is removed, the remaining 30 percent enlarges to a mass as big as the original in a compensatory feat.

Somehow the ancients must have known of the liver's unique ability, which perhaps gave rise to the Greek myth around the punishment of Prometheus. When the Titan god offended Zeus, the supreme deity, Zeus chained the rebellious Prometheus to a boulder and dispatched an eagle to eat his liver each day. Each night the organ regrew, and the bird would return to consume it over and over again. Prometheus's crime had been to bring the human race a gift that was supposed to be reserved for the gods. The gift was fire.

As he pushed his regeneration inquiry further, Yannas also began working with people who were looking for commercial backing to develop the artificial skin. It was necessary to move to larger-scale clinical tests on real patients to prove to regulators at the Food and Drug Administration, which must approve all new medical devices, that it would work. Yannas recalled that "platoons" of MBAs and salespeople from large pharmaceutical companies came to his lab to see the artificial skin and gauge its potential. "You realize that the burn market is very small," said one visiting rep one day.

"Fortunately, yes," Yannas responded.

"Well, we can't justify investment."

"I told the interested parties that the skin also had potential for cosmetic surgery procedures," Yannas recalled. The forecast did not seem to impress them.

Finally, in the early 1980s, one company bit. Marion Laboratories of Kansas City, Missouri, was marketing Silvadene, an anti-bacterial cream widely used to treat wounds in burn patients. Marion thought it could market the artificial skin product using the same sales force and selling to the same surgeons. After Marion acquired licensing rights from MIT, it set up a plan for its development and eventually gave it the name Integra.

Yannas went to Missouri to help consult on the large-scale development of his artificial skin. Marion had spent most of the decade and millions of dollars to get the skin ready for market—when the company was suddenly acquired by Dow Chemical. It was precisely at the time that Dow Corning, an affiliated company, was mired in billions of dollars of litigation from women claiming its silicone breast implants were unsafe. Dow Corning denied that charge, but it eventually exited the breast-implant business and agreed in the early 1990s to pay $2 billion into a global settlement of claims against its silicone device.

Thus in the new corporate ownership, nervousness around liability was a first strike against Integra. Because the artificial skin was a medical device—much more complex than a pill—surgeons would have to be trained by company sales reps in the best techniques for applying the product. That would take a fairly sophisticated sales force, capable of showing skilled surgeons how to operate. On top of that difficulty, Yannas said, lawyers for Marion Merrell Dow, as the company came to be called, were having difficulty quantifying the liability risk for Integra—something very much on their minds with the massive breast-implant litigation pending.

A clinical trial in a highly respected burn unit at Harborview Medical Center in Seattle, led by Dr. David Heimbach, was showing great success in treating severely burned patients with the artificial skin. The factory in Missouri was being readied. And Marion Labs had submitted an application to the FDA around the time of its 1989 acquisition by Dow. The application was based primarily on the published data from clinical trials that Dr. Burke had defended before colleagues in Chicago a few years earlier.

But amid the breast-implant woes and the new corporate parent's wishes, Marion Merrell Dow suddenly pulled the plug on the Integra project. Charles Blitzer, who was the company's vice president for licensing and business development at the time, was involved in the corporate analysis. After the acquisition he recalled, "I was one of a team of seven that was asked to do the strategic plan for MMD out ten years. Strategically the burn/wound business was simply too small to invest in, and the anticipated return-on-investment against the rest of the combined businesses of Marion and Merrell Dow was paltry.

"When you go from being a billion-dollar business [Marion at the time of the merger] and $20 million to $25 million is your burn/wound care segment, to being a $2 billion-plus business post the merger, strategically and financially, during a strategic planning process you must ask whether the burn-open wound business makes any sense at all. Answer: no."

Lita Nelsen, who was then director of the technology licensing office for MIT, remembers calling Dow at the time. "I expressed to them our dismay that this potentially life-saving technology would sit on the shelf . . . after the acquisition. This would neither be good public policy nor good 'human' policy."

And Yanni Yannas, his thick curls by now greying, was inconsolable: "I saw twenty years of work grind to a halt."

5

WAKING UP

At length his senses were overpowered, his eyes
swam in his head, his head gradually declined,
and he fell into a deep sleep. . . .
On waking [twenty years later] he rubbed his
eyes. "Surely," thought Rip, "I have not slept here
all night."

—Washington Irving, "Rip van Winkle"

ON Valentine's Day 2000, after dinner, Rhoda went to the hospital's burn-support group again. Listening to the people air their anxieties, she couldn't help thinking about finances. Within days Rhoda met with a lawyer to discuss medical bills. "I think all will be OK—will work with U. of W. a bit, and if all else fails declare bankruptcy," she wrote. She particularly felt Ted's absence around financial matters. "I really miss Ted and his ability to always know what to do."

Ted had spent years fashioning himself into a small businessman, a fiercely proud do-it-yourselfer. He wore greasy overalls by day, but at night, with the glow of the computer monitor in his face, he watched overseas agriculture markets to see where prices were headed.

After the accident, a fund was established in Lanark at the Exchange State Bank. Newspaper ads, with art showing a heart and a bow, noted that collections were being taken for "Ted Fink who was burned in an LP accident. All his medical insurance has been exhausted. Any donations would be greatly appreciated."

In farm communities the letters LP need no explanation. They stand for liquid petroleum, or propane. The most common form of liquid fuel, propane is used on more than 600,000 farms across the country to run irrigation pumps, emergency generators, grain dryers, and other farm equipment. It is 270 times more compact as a liquid than as a gas.

It came about because of a fluke. In 1910 Dr. Walter O. Snelling, a chemist and explosives expert for the U.S. Bureau of Mines, was investigating why vapors were emanating from the gasoline tank of a Ford Model T. He bottled up the mysterious gas in a glass jug and took it back to his lab. The cork kept popping off. In tinkering with the vaporous gases, he found that the propane portion could be controlled and used as fuel for cooking ranges, metal-cutting blowtorches, and lanterns. A propane industry was born.

Ted Fink had worked with propane his whole life. On the fateful Saturday in November 1999, as the details finally became clear to accident investigators, he was moving a thousand-gallon tank of propane. Shuttling such tanks was a routine chore. On that day, though, the chain that held the tank to his tractor snapped. The tank tumbled to the ground and began leaking. Then in a bizarre accident, the tractor apparently backfired, igniting the gas and causing it to explode.

Such explosions, momentarily as blinding as the sun, can appear apocalyptic. They are called boiling liquid expanding vapor explosions. As tanks burst apart, metal pieces and other projectiles may be propelled half a mile. At the Fink farm the explosion produced a flash that neighbors on nearby farms said they saw as far as three miles away. There was also a thunderous rumble, then the ball of flame. Ted Fink was in the middle of it.

Safely ensconced in room No. 5 at the burn unit in Madison, Ted was undergoing surgery about every ten days, often for skin grafts. Through IV tubes he was taking fluids, antibiotics, and morphine. Occasionally his eyes would simply open while he was comatose, and doctors had to sew his eyelids shut so his eyes would not dry out and damage his corneas.

Early on he had swollen up, as many victims of severe burns do. He resembled the lumpy, tire-stacked Michelin Man. A burn triggers a blitzkrieg of immune and inflammatory responses within the body, which struggles to maintain a semblance of equilibrium between fluid levels, blood pressure, body temperature, and metabolism. The body can quickly become starved as the need for energy to repair wounds and reconstruct damaged tissue soars.

Dr. Schurr kept draping Ted's body in Integra, which solved a life-threatening problem. Someone burned as badly as Ted typically lacks enough healthy skin to "harvest" thin slices to replace burned spots. The Integra allowed Dr. Schurr to cover immediately the head-to-ankle open wound Ted had become. It gave Ted precious time to regenerate skin from his few unburned spots for grafts. The lower layer of Integra substitutes for the dermis, the lower level of skin, but doctors still must graft the victim's own epidermis on top of it.

Dr. Schurr had to scavenge hard for good skin on Ted's body. The surgeon took thin slices from his unburned feet and armpits. The so-called harvested skin can be meshed and stretched to cover a spot larger than the original donor site. Some skin was sent to a lab in Boston to grow even larger pieces called cultured skin.

For Dr. Schurr, Ted was one of the most severely burned patients he had encountered—but not the most publicized. A year and a half before Ted's accident, Eric Nelson and Heather Gallagher, an engaged couple in their twenties, had hopped aboard a city bus in Madison after a shopping trip one day. A man suddenly boarded the bus with a bucket of gasoline, doused Nelson, and struck a match. In all, five people on the Madison Metro bus were burned. The flames left Nelson and his fiancée burned over more than 80 percent of their bodies. The following year the fire setter, who had told police he heard strange voices in his head, was committed to a mental institution for 104 years. The Madison media followed every step of the couple's story, including their discharge months later from the hospital and their wedding, which had been postponed a full year. For a time Madisonians wore blue ribbons in support of the bus victims.

In relative obscurity, Ted recovered slowly in Madison. His new skin was incrementally beginning to fill in. As Rhoda put it, "his back has some small islands of skin." But her anxiety about Ted's being weaned off his sedatives, still months away, continued. "I'm really scared about what Ted will say and think when he's awake. . . ." One day after lugging her laundry home to Lanark from Madison, she heard of another community effort to raise money for the family. She appreciated the gesture, but the Finks were fiercely independent and asked no one for assistance. She confided to her diary, "I also wish everyone would NOT do the fundraisers. They just make me embarrassed."

As the weeks passed and Ted slept, Rhoda began clipping his toenails and fingernails, an intimacy she noted each time in her diary. Occupational therapists began putting splints on Ted's fingers and employing tension wires to bend them, to keep them from stiffening up.

With no outer skin, Ted was missing the delicate layer of insulation that regulates temperature. His body could not keep itself warm, so the nurses cranked up the heat in the room and laid thermal blankets on top of him. At one point they put ice on the thermostat. Rhoda felt nauseated, spending so much time in that sauna. She had to retreat frequently. "They are still keeping Ted's room hot—around 85 degrees. I can only stay with him about forty minutes, then have to go cool off. I just want to wake him up and take him home."

The therapists came routinely and used rubber bands and the splints to restore some flexibility to his rigid fingers. Sometimes swelling set in in unexpected places. One morning, after a night of swelling, Ted's tongue became too big for his mouth and poked out between his teeth. "Looks awful," Rhoda wrote. That day a local paper in Illinois, the *Freeport Journal-Standard*, asked Ted's sister Judy for an update on how her brother was doing. About as well as could be expected, she said.

The next day a benefit was held in Lanark for the Fink family. Student leaders at Eastland High School had organized a pancake breakfast fund-raiser for early March. They were helped by members of the school's Future Farmers of America club. From seven in the morning until one in the afternoon, students in the cafeteria served French toast, cinnamon rolls, orange juice, pancakes, eggs, and sausage. There was no charge; only donations were accepted. A scheduling conflict caused the Community Boosters group in the nearby town of Chadwick to cancel its pancake breakfast planned for the same Saturday. The group decided to have a ham supper benefit later in the month.

On that sunny Saturday, when it was an unseasonable 70 degrees for March, about 1,200 people showed up for the Fink fund-raiser—nearly every man, woman, and child in Lanark. The event raised some $14,600. "Just seeing everyone come yesterday was a great example of how much community spirit there is for families in need," Peter Fink told a newspaper reporter afterward. The story carried the headline, "Community Rallies Around Burn Victim." Rhoda made an appearance, answered some questions about Ted's condition, and then, after making a wrong turn along the way, drove back to Madison.

By this time doctors had removed the stitches from Ted's eyes. One morning Rhoda came into his room to find Ted staring from his bed, wide-eyed. He was there, but he wasn't. She found it eerie and tried to focus on things outside the room. "Talked to bed 4's wife, Cherie. She seems nice. Has little kids. Hubby burned in electric box flash fire. Will be OK."

A couple of days later, Rhoda's maternal instincts were triggered. Back at the farm the boys were planning to burn tree stumps they had dug up. "I hope the burning tomorrow goes OK. God, I worry—especially with fire." She sat with Ted and shared her concerns with her comatose husband. She prayed for her sons at church later that night, and after dinner at Red Lobster with friends who were visiting, she returned to the burn unit and heard details of the latest person admitted: a twenty-three-year-old man brought from Rockford with 55 to 60 percent of his body burned, mostly from the waist up.

The commute between Lanark and Madison grew tiresome, but Rhoda needed to get home now and then to check on the boys and the farm, and to do her laundry. Returning to Madison one Monday morning, she was put off by traffic. "I'm really getting to HATE big-city life," Rhoda wrote. "Ready to go home. If I could, I'd load Ted up in the car and head out of here."

Phoning the boys from the hospital one night, she learned that Chris had burned his face in a grass fire. Looking at her dormant husband, she turned to her reliable confessor, the diary. "BURNED his FACE," she wrote. "That was the last straw. I achieved melt down. Cry Cry Cry. I miss Ted so much. I want to talk to him so much." One of the nurses tried to console her, unsuccessfully, and Rhoda left for the basement apartment "where I rant and rave and cry, cry, cry. It's getting harder and harder as time goes by, not easier. What am I supposed to be doing? I don't know. . . ."

By the time she and Ted had spent 135 days in the burn unit, it was early April 2000. Ted was restless in his bed. His skin was filling in nicely. Infection was under control. The doctors were talking about weaning him off his breathing machine, a step toward reviving him. Again Rhoda was apprehensive. She had had months to adjust to how he looked, his physical infirmities, the loss of his thumb. What would *he* think?

"I worry a lot about how all this will come out. How much will Ted be able to do, walk, talk, eat? Will he be able to farm in some capacity?"

At home the First Lutheran Church in the town of Chadwick, near Lanark, held a soup benefit on a Sunday in early April and raised $5,970. Rhoda went to the burn-support group the next night. She spoke with Ted's sister, Judy, and re-layed the latest plans to wake Ted up. In her basement apartment the next evening she ate leftover chili from the church benefit and wrote out Easter cards. A few nights later, after dinner with visiting friends at an Olive Garden restaurant, Rhoda broke down. "Cried and cried," she wrote. "I miss Ted— talking to him, holding him, hugging, cuddling, etc."

At the farm, Chris began planting sweet corn, the kind that people eat on the cob. One problem farmers have with their sweet corn is that raccoons find it tasty. And the animals often have a way of knowing just when it's ripe and making a small feast for themselves. It wouldn't be so troublesome if the critters gorged on an ear or two, but they like to nibble just a few kernels from one ear, then move on to the next. Some people try putting radios in their sweet-corn gardens, to scare the raccoons away. But Rhoda's experience had sug-gested otherwise. A radio merely provided, as she said, "din-ner music."

Planting season was in full swing, and on a Saturday af-ternoon Rhoda drove by an orchard that Ted had planted many years earlier. The pear, cherry, and apple trees were just beginning to bloom. It was precisely the time that Ted loved to visit the orchard each year, to smell the intoxicating aromas of a new growing season. Ted liked to be part of something the ancient Persian poet Hafiz once called "the spring orchestra of scents."

In Madison Rhoda received an unwelcome surprise. After repeated tussles over the phone, the woman from whom she had been renting the basement apartment had decided to evict her. The landlady frowned on Rhoda's answering the phone—even if the lady of the house was out—but Rhoda had given the phone number to the hospital so she could be reached in an emergency. And every time the house's only phone rang, Rhoda wondered. Calls to Lanark were long distance, which did not set well with the landlady either.

"Boy, will I write her a letter," Rhoda wrote in her diary that night. "I'm ragged out—the basement was too good to be true. Don't know what I'll do. She gave me a month, but I won't stay where I'm not wanted. I'll stay one more week."

The hospital provided a list of people with available housing for families of patients on extended stay, but Rhoda's rental had stretched not just weeks but months, with no end in sight. She debated spending money on a hotel room versus the cost of gasoline for commuting between Madison and Lanark. The next night she reflected, "I was beginning to hate that cold, musty hole. The bed and bath were both terrible." Around this time she visited an Illinois public aid office in Mt. Carroll, near Lanark. She filled out paperwork for Ted to receive Medicaid payments. Later she went to the bank to speak with Bart Ottens, the officer who helped her and Ted with loans for the farm, year in and year out. They discussed remortgaging the Fink farm to provide some cash. It was a huge step, and one she was certain Ted, ultraconservative with finances, would not be happy about. "Yes, I can hear Ted screaming," she wrote that night. "But I don't want the hospital to get the farm in the end."

After commuting between Illinois and Wisconsin for several days, in late April Rhoda decided to take a room at the Ivy Inn in Madison. Chris continued planting corn. Doctors at the burn unit became concerned about the poorly healing index finger on Ted's right hand, his dominant one and the one from which he had already lost a thumb. Rhoda told the boys about it over spaghetti she made at home that night.

Raised as a Lutheran, with a view of gambling as sinful, Rhoda found herself picking up a five-dollar lottery ticket in Lanark the following Saturday when she heard the jackpot had reached $200 million. The boys went on planting.

One night the Ivy Inn smelled musty to Rhoda, so she packed up her clothes and belongings and checked into the Best Western where she had stayed the first night of Ted's accident. That was 176 days earlier. "Wake him up! Get him off the ventilator! I want to be home for Christmas for God's sake."

The following Sunday Rhoda decided to skip church— "I'm beginning to really not want to go there." She stayed home to clean out a closet and iron some of Ted's shirts. The next day her pastor called to check on her, and read a little inspirational passage. "The 'thought for the day' was a verse from Deuteronomy reminding me to be duly thankful," she griped into her diary. "Gee—I'll try to do that. . . . Ted needs to wake up for Rhoda's mental health."

During the third week of May, as the leaves on the honey locust tree sprouted greenish-yellow blossoms, the doctors carefully eased Ted off sedatives and his breathing apparatus. One of the nurses asked Ted to open his mouth so she could clean it out. He did. Out of her habit of talking to her patients while she treated them, the nurse asked, "Ted, am I torturing you?" This time he shook his head side to side. The nurse and Rhoda screamed and hugged each other. He was regaining consciousness.

Within days the eye doctors decided it would be best for the protection of Ted's eyes to sew them shut again. Nurses continued to wean him from the ventilator. Progress was slow but evident. Having been out of it for nearly two hundred days, Ted might be completely conscious within weeks. The weight of that change began to produce anxiety for Rhoda. "I worry about the quality of life issues," she wrote on a drizzly Tuesday in Madison. "Hope he can farm in some capacity and won't hate me."

Rhoda liked spending more time in Lanark but had to come to grips with Ted's being in the hospital for several more months. Reluctantly she phoned around and found a sublet in student housing on the University of Wisconsin campus. She took room No. 34 in Allen House, showing up with clothes, bed linens, and a TV. It was Spartan, though: no dishes, pots, or pans. Her room was by the front door, and she could hear constant foot traffic, stereos, and the hoots and howls of partying students.

After his head-nodding with the nurse, Ted was not particularly responsive, but Rhoda kept talking to him just the same. "I'm just not sure how much he hears and understands.

Makes it so hard when he gets frustrated and agitated," her diary entry recorded.

Over those months Rhoda worried too about her weight. Eating out took its toll. On the first Saturday of June her diary entry read: "Connie, RN, comes into the waiting room and tells me Ted's crying, upset, asking for me, etc. Says I should get into scrubs and climb into bed with him. Sounds good, but I'm too big—scrubs and bed too small. So I just lean over and talk to him."

The rest of the month Ted continued a slow ascent into awareness. On a sunny Saturday in mid-July, when he was stirring in his deep sleep, Rhoda recalled sitting at his bedside and telling him she loved him, as she had many times before. On this day, though, he squeezed her hand lightly three times. "A real sign to me," she wrote later in her diary. At the top of the page she noted that the corn back home was in that romantic phase her young boyfriend had told her about years earlier out in the fields.

In the diary she wrote, "Corn is tasseling."

Rhoda was talking to her unresponsive husband again the next Sunday, telling him that the two neighbors who saved him had been nominated for a recognition called a Carnegie Hero Award. It was given to people who met stringent criteria for risking their lives in extraordinary ways. It carried a cash bonus. She told Ted she hoped they would win it.

After driving to the farm and checking the corn, which looked mostly good to her, she returned to the hospital. She wanted some indication that Ted knew she was there, and in exasperation she barked, "Give me a sign." He slowly raised both arms. Rhoda was heartened, but she could see he was still "pretty fogged in."

At Allen House, Rhoda had begun lifting three-pound weights and working out to a Richard Simmons video. At the hospital, Chris began bringing his new girlfriend, Deanna, when he came to visit. The nurses were now sitting Ted in a chair periodically, but he remained mostly unresponsive, and Rhoda felt her dream of having Ted home by Christmas slipping away. Was she going to be alone with her Snowbabies figurines collection again this year?

Every few days Ted tried to speak, but it was just mumbling, and Rhoda was petrified that the moment he finally could utter something she would not be there to hear it. Or he would awaken, find her not there, and assume she had not stayed by his side. "I think he's more aware than we think. Just can't communicate," she wrote. "I hate the thought of that. I hate to leave him."

On a Sunday in mid-July, Rhoda attended "Ted Fink Day" at a church in Chadwick. The benefit included a silent auction, an ice cream social, and karaoke. Chris was there with her. More than 650 people showed up. Rhoda put on a good face: the appreciative victim's wife. "I'm still embarrassed," she wrote when she was out of the spotlight later that night. "Ted would hate it."

Nearly a week later the nurses sat Ted up in a chair around eleven in the morning. It was his 246th day in the hospital. They changed the little plug in his neck for his breathing tube, and Ted rasped out a few sounds that once again resembled words. But these were somewhat clearer. They sounded purposeful. He really was trying to say something.

Rhoda and the nurses leaned in. What was he trying to say? The nurses looked at Rhoda, but she couldn't make it out either. She shook her head, and they began mimicking the movement of his lips, trying to figure out what Ted was saying, as if trying to give volume and clarity to what was on the lips of the awakening patient. Slowly it became clearer. Ted was reciting names. Slowly Rhoda could begin to make out "Peter," "Chris," "Don," "Judy," "Rhoda."

Then, within moments, in Ted's first coherent sentence, he rasped three words through his breathing tube:

"What . . . will . . . change?"

6

HOME FOR CHRISTMAS

❦ GRATEFUL for the first evidence that her husband's mind had not vanished in the fire, Rhoda pondered his question from that July day in 2000.

What *will* change?

"Boy, did I talk to him. Tell him all will be OK. Later he also gave me a hug and a kiss. Well, I had to cry. He's beginning to understand what is up with his condition," Rhoda confided to her diary.

After 246 days of abandonment, she suddenly found herself in the odd position of having Ted back—nearly, but having through necessity grown closer to her diary through her raw and honest outpouring. Her candor had become sharper in what she wrote for herself than in what she said to others, particularly the man drifting in and out of awareness and their lives.

In a matter of days Ted went from silence to incoherent chatter. He found himself talking up a nurse named Kelly, who was surprised when he insisted that he was in a hospital in New Jersey. Rhoda could not figure out where that came from—maybe because Peter had just been at a computer conference in New Jersey—but she was convinced that Ted was otherwise "with it." One afternoon plastic surgeons came by to look at his right hand and said something that startled Rhoda. They suggested they could make a new thumb for him.

It was late July, just days after asking "What will change?," and Ted was talking to Peter about college and his car. Through his questions it became clear that Ted was confused—he thought it was still 1999. Ted had lost track of about seven months of his life.

It was a page straight out of Washington Irving's whimsical tale of Rip van Winkle, the colonial slouch who ventured out one night with his little dog and, after heavy drinking, fell sound asleep. When he awoke, he came to learn that he had not merely slept overnight but for two solid decades, missing the American Revolution and the installation of Congress and President George Washington.

There was much to tell Ted. During his months in a coma, he had not only missed the mass hysteria around Y2K but also the pageantry, celebrations, and momentous media coverage of the close of the twentieth century. A governor from Texas with a familiar name, George Bush, had wrested the Republican party nomination from other contenders. The First Lady, Hillary Clinton, with her husband a scandalized lame duck in the White House, had declared that she would run for a U.S. Senate seat in New York. A Concorde jet had crashed near Paris, killing all 109 aboard, in the first crash since the supersonic jet began commercial operation in 1976. And a little Cuban boy—trapped in a tug-of-war between relatives in Miami and a father from Castro's Cuba—had captured the attention of the country for several months. It was not until summer, after armed immigration officers had stormed the Miami house where the boy had been staying with family, that the courts finally allowed the Cuban father to take back his son, Elian Gonzalez.

Beyond giving her husband a refresher course in current affairs, Rhoda had graver concerns: Ted had yet to see his new self in a mirror. What's more, there were harsh realities about his remaining physical abilities. "I worry that Ted, the big, strong, in-control, smart, mind-sharp guy is so reduced to 'invalid' status. I just pray and pray that he will get back to what he was before. . . .

"I worry about his reaction to his face, hands, body, etc. . . . I told him how long he had been here, etc. The farm doesn't seem to be a big worry, which surprised me."

A doctor came by one afternoon and, after examining Ted, told Rhoda that nerve damage in his arm would affect his ability to move his wrist. Rhoda had been hoping that Ted was on the road to improvement and that the worst was behind them. "By God, Ted," she wrote, "we saved you, but you can't *do* anything! I hope not."

She also reflected, "Talked to Ted about his right hand. He tells me, 'I don't have to farm.' Breaks my heart. . . ."

The next day doctors reviewed x-rays of Ted's right hand and told the couple it did not look good for Ted's troubled index finger. Trying to ease Rhoda into the emotional trials that Ted faced, the hospital gave her some burn-victim videotapes. "Gives me much to think about," she wrote. "How Ted will do, think, feel as he heals."

Ted Fink's first real food since the accident consisted of Gerber strained pears, mashed potatoes, and a carton of milk.

He asked for a doughnut. All signs were that he was moving toward normalcy, and nurses suddenly grew concerned that it would be only a matter of time before he wanted to see himself. No one mentioned a mirror.

"Ted's face looks good to me—very different, of course, but one I can love. I hope Ted can get used to it over time," Rhoda wrote. Hospital bills arrived for June and July—$145,000 and $99,000, respectively. Rhoda could not wait for the tracheotomy device in Ted's neck to be removed. It made it hard to understand what he was saying, and she lamented that she was not a lip-reader. There were things she had yet to tell him, and she felt compelled to. "Need to talk to Ted about how sick he was and how far he's come."

One morning Rhoda fed her husband breakfast and brushed his teeth, and they kissed afterward. For her it was sorely missed affection.

Rhoda had gotten into a routine of visiting with Ted Monday through Friday, then going home to Lanark on weekends. There she luxuriated in her own bed, fed the boys, visited with her mother, ran errands, and opened stacks of piled-up mail. The daily habit of journaling, so salving while Ted was in a coma, turned to a more mundane chronicling of car washes, laundry-doing, and dinners at Applebee's and Red Lobster. She noted who had sent a card or a donation, griped about overstaying or unannounced visitors, and worried about bills. As in a farmer's almanac, daily weather conditions were recorded religiously.

On a Sunday in late August, eighty-six degrees and humid, Rhoda made the trek to Madison and was greeted by Connie, one of the nurses, who said Ted had been calling for her, missing her. Rhoda sensed it was the moment for a long-overdue heart-to-heart.

"Ted and I talked a lot," she wrote that night. "He remembers the accident and tells me he was in the tractor and bailed out after it backfired. Tells me he was 'stupid' and did a 'dumb thing.' He cried, sobbed, and said he felt like crying a lot. I tell him that's OK to do. I tell him how bad he was burned and how the kids and I agonized over the life-and-death decisions. I tell him things will get better, and with time he'll get back on track. Tells me he's sorry for putting me through all this. Says he shouldn't miss me so much.

"I feel so bad for him at this stage. He's aware, but he's helpless."

When Ted's sister Judy visited the next day, she arrived with popcorn from the Carroll County Fair, something Ted loved to attend as a boy. Childhood memories can come wafting back with certain sensations of youth—the scent of waxy crayons or the gritty crunch of popcorn.

The county fair of 1965 had opened with everyone talking about that eleven-year-old Ted. At his early age he had boldly entered the tractor-pull event. He wanted to be the driver who hauled that massive, stubborn load of concrete bars the farthest—and take home the trophy. He had studied the poor performers, the ones who spun tires and kicked up dust and gravel and barely moved the load. Sometimes their engines, racing loudly, burned out, leaving the befuddled contestant in a cloud of sooty smoke. Mistimed gearshifts made the front tires of their tractors jerk upward, losing traction and potential distance. It got harder as weight was added to the concrete "sled" as the tractor moved along. Often it was human weight—progressively more men or boys stepping onto the concrete blocks every few feet. They all were pulled along like waving beauties in a parade float.

The blond boy had practiced and practiced on the farm, straining the machine to its fullest capacity. Ted had ridden tractors since he was five. Sometimes he lay awake at night, figuring out how to get the peak performance from his Massey Ferguson. He seemed to be a natural at this rural sport. But all was just bluster and boast until one actually stepped into the ring at the Carroll County Fair.

When the Tuesday night he had dreamed about finally arrived, Ted looked like a small man in the large tractor. He wore a straw-rimmed hat and a crisp white short-sleeve shirt. His head just above the steering wheel, he looked from side to side between the twin, over-size tires. At one point, as he inched along at one to two miles an hour, the front end of the tractor bucked upward under the strain, and the packed crowds in the grandstands cheered on the towheaded tractor-pull prodigy. He pulled on the gearshift and pressed the pedals just so, navigating more than 11,000 pounds more than 125 feet before stopping. The load included a light tractor, four large cement blocks, and several tanned boys.

The feat, by one so young, made the papers across northern Illinois and even as far away as Iowa. "An eleven-year-old lad outranked the men in the first event at the tractor pulling contest at the County Fair," began one account. "Ted Fink, Lanark, entered in the men's event, driving tractors up to 6,000 pounds, drove off with the first-place award." He even beat his Uncle Vernon, who finished sixth.

At the hospital the popcorn, the memories, and Judy all proved welcome diversions. Judy had a light touch that helped snap the dark days for Rhoda. Judy's message on her answering machine at home said, "We can't come to the phone. We're either out farming, or baking cakes." In no time Rhoda and Judy were laughing about some memory or some quirk at the hospital. "No need to cry," Judy said later. "It just makes you tired."

In the burn unit the day Judy brought the popcorn, an eighty-year-old man died from burns over 85 percent of his body. The next day another man was brought in to bed No. 6 with an 85 percent burn. And the man in bed No. 3 had somehow managed to burn his penis, and only that.

Ted could stand for the first time, unaided, on a Tuesday in early August. He stayed up for four minutes. This was progress. Physical therapists had been putting Ted on a tilt table, which helps people who have been bedridden for a long time to readjust to being upright again—slowly and at incrementally increasing angles from horizontal to vertical. The table helps reacquaint the human body, its reflexes and muscles and sense of balance, with gravity.

One of the surgeons examined Ted's right hand again on a Sunday in mid-August and privately told Rhoda, as she put it in her own words, the "index finger is a goner. . . . Got me depressed. Must talk to Ted about it in a calm moment."

As the hot summer wore on, Rhoda became aware that Ted's recovery, then approaching its fortieth week, was not close to ending. His index finger remained an issue, and the skin on his back was not filling in properly. He could barely stand. Rhoda had long since stopped joking about how the breathing machine, after all the bills the Finks had paid, be-longed to them. She recalled how long Eric Nelson, the young man burned in the freak bus fire, had been at the burn unit. "Eric went home after 50 weeks—No way will we manage that. I just feel so bad for Ted. I still hope he doesn't hate me for saving him."

The next Tuesday, at 10:45 in the morning, Ted left for the operating room. One doctor did a skin graft on the back of his head. Another amputated his right index finger.

Ted began spending more time on the tilt table, and he started using a special airbed to help the fragile skin on his back heal more quickly. Rehabilitation of his arms, hands, and feet was set to begin October 1, a month later, and Rhoda saw the calendar getting away from her. "I just wanted to be home by Christmas—not Valentine's Day."

One Thursday in early September, Rhoda ordered roses as a thank-you to the organizer of one of the benefits in Illinois. After lunch Ted stood on his own for eight minutes and began to shuffle his feet a bit, as a prelude to walking again. He finally had enough wispy white babylike hairs growing from the back of his head that Rhoda got some scissors and clipped them.

When she finished, she looked at her husband's face. Without his saying a word she could tell what he was thinking, and she began to get a sinking feeling. He was quiet for a time. She did not relax. Then he finally asked for a mirror.

Rhoda paused and then handed him one, and Ted looked at himself. Later that night Rhoda recounted in her diary what happened. "Doesn't say much at first. Then he says, 'Who could love anybody that looks like this?' Oh boy, more talking and crying. Tell him I love him no matter what. . . . Ted gets all upset over his face, ears, etc. I tell him we all love him for what's inside and it will be OK. . . . Ted says he looks like a freak. I tell him if folks don't like it, they can go to hell."

When the hospital scheduled a big picnic for burn survivors and their families, Rhoda found herself too worn out from the mirror episode to make her Jell-O dish. Ted got so discouraged he could not sleep. He was afraid to sleep, worried about nightmares. He felt anxious and restless. Rhoda went to the picnic and saw Eric and Heather Nelson, the celebrity burn couple, as well as people from her burn-support group. A teenage boy arrived in the burn unit on the Sunday of the picnic, burned over 30 percent of his body after a homemade bomb exploded.

At Day 300 in the hospital, Rhoda noted that the Summer Olympics had begun, halfway around the world in Sydney, Australia. While the world's finest athletes ran and swam, for the first time Ted walked to the door using a walker and escorted by physical therapists. He turned around and then walked back to his bed. "Hard work for him," Rhoda observed, "but a real milestone in his recovery." Nurses told her later that he was crying about the three-hundred-day anniversary. "He seems to cry a lot and he sits, and he worries about everything."

A few days later, as autumn approached, Rhoda went shopping and picked up a new Snowbabies ornament, though it had been so long since she paid attention to her collection that she could not recall if she already owned it. Homesick, she returned to Lanark for the weekend. To her diary she said: "Home to find boys combining, and grain dryers running. Man, do I miss the farm! My house! My bed! My washer! My kitchen! Did laundry, fixed a chicken dinner."

Wounds on Ted's back still were not healing properly, so the doctors tried an old remedy: pigskin. It can often be used as a temporary dressing, but it will not "take" as a replacement skin because the body's immune system rejects the flesh as foreign.

A few days later it was Rhoda's birthday, and Judy arrived with a cake, candles, and a gift from Ted, a Black Hills gold pendant. Rhoda was grateful but would have preferred new Snowbabies or, better still, progress on Ted's back. The pigskin was not working, so rehab had to be postponed.

"Feel about at the end of my rope," Rhoda reflected. "I'm in the middle of a F—ing mess, and I don't see much hope for being home by Christmas. I don't know if I can manage much more."

Just two days later, as if sensing her despair, Ted got up, leaned on his walker, and somehow managed to do a slow lap around the circular burn unit. Depending on where someone was in the hallway, a wall might obstruct the view so that the patient could not be seen from the nurses' station. As a joke, a nurse named Mike had Ted, a well-known and longtime resident, paged: "Ted Fink—please report to the burn unit. Repeat, Ted Fink, please report to the burn unit." When he returned to the room, Ted brought a can of Dr Pepper for Rhoda. He had bought it at the vending machine and strapped it to his walker.

Halloween fell on a Tuesday; a few trick-or-treaters came through the burn unit. One of the longtime nurses, Cindy, noted that Rhoda had "lived" in the burn unit with Ted for nearly a year at that point. She and others found

Rhoda to be a cheerful addition, an unofficial welcome wagon for the new "admits."

Starting to sense the gathering progress, Rhoda broke from her routine and drove to the farm on a weekday, a Thursday, for some of the last combining of the season. She rode with Peter. She stopped in Freeport to visit with her mother, then got some books and clothes at J. C. Penney and drove back to Madison.

Election day brought her back to Lanark on a weekday the following week. She stayed up late to watch the election returns, but the race between George Bush and Al Gore was too close to call in the early morning hours. Same thing the next morning. Both candidates, and the country, awaited the verdict.

Rhoda finally had national company in her impatience. As tallies were recounted in Florida, Rhoda and Ted talked about whether they might simply skip the rehabilitation procedures and head home. "What would rehab do for us?" she asked her diary. "I think it would be just more practice and we can do that at home. Christmas is looking better all the time."

Then Rhoda became torn. "We still are having big discussions about rehab or not-to-rehab. Ted really wants to go home. So do I, but not before we are ready. Ted HAS to be able to do a few things for himself. Bathroom, eat, in and out of bed and chair. Yikes!" It was November 16, a little more than a week after the election, and the presidential race was still unsettled.

"Ted keeps talking about going home—and soon. I'm not sure how we will manage," Rhoda worried. "Ted doesn't have a clue as to what needs to transpire before we can do this. Mostly, it makes me way nervous."

It was thirty-five degrees in Lanark on Thanksgiving Day. This was the second Thanksgiving for Ted in the hospital, but Rhoda could see the end approaching. She got to bed early on Wednesday night, with plans to carve turkey with her mother in Freeport the next day. She planned to call Madison to wish Ted a happy Thanksgiving and check on him, but the hospital called first. Overnight Ted's temperature had risen; he appeared to have developed pneumonia. They immediately put him on three strong antibiotics and carefully checked his lungs.

"This takes care of him coming home by Christmas," Rhoda wrote. "Now there is no way to get him healthy and strong by then. . . . I really don't understand the 'why' of all this, and especially this last turn of events. I probably want to go home too much, or I'm not praying right, enough, or good enough. . . . I'm about to give up. Hopefully, Ted won't."

Through the weekend it was touch-and-go. The doctors put the tracheotomy tube back in his throat, and Ted was again on a breathing machine. "A big step backward for me," thought Rhoda. "I thought those days were gone forever." Ted's condition worsened: his blood pressure fell, his breathing was poor. He was suffering from sepsis, a potentially lethal poisoning of the blood that sometimes follows surgery. He was given two units of blood. Frightened, Rhoda called Judy and her mother and Peter. She raced back to Madison. "I thought he was goners," she recalled.

By noon Saturday, Ted could talk and seemed greatly improved, but his kidneys were estimated to be working at only about 14 percent efficiency, Rhoda recalled. Despite all the progress Ted had made, Rhoda had a sinking feeling he was approaching death, and she desperately wanted to talk to him. "Ted tries to talk but it's impossible with the vent. So frustrating to try to talk to him." She went outside and cried. "I'm tired, disappointed, discouraged and depressed. Hope they don't need to do dialysis on Ted."

The next day everything had improved but his kidneys. If his toxin levels did not improve in the next twenty-four to thirty-six hours, Ted would have to go on dialysis. He was at the doorstep of a level of disability that Rhoda, having worked her whole adult life in hospitals, dreaded.

"God, the fun just never stops," she wrote. "It's just not fair that we've come so far together and then get shot down like this."

After minimal improvement the next day, Rhoda thought, "Christmas will be a non-event again this year. That's what I hate the most: My life being on hold for 12 to 15 months."

Then, for no discernible reason, doctors were surprised to find that Ted's kidneys began incrementally improving. When he was finally in the clear by the following Wednesday, Rhoda collapsed in emotion and thought: "I wish Ted could hold me and give me some support, but he doesn't have anything to spare. Cried all the way to the apartment. Not a fun time here."

Even the next day she remained in despair. "Ted says he's tired of it all. I don't blame him a bit. . . . I just feel so bad for Ted and all he's going through. Will I ever get my bear back?"

When December began, that Friday, her thoughts turned again to the elusive seasonal holiday. "I don't think I want to do Christmas this year."

Christmas Day 2000 was bitter cold in Lanark—twenty-one degrees below zero that morning. By noon it warmed to ten degrees. Peter and Chris and his girlfriend Deanna, along with Rhoda and her mother, spent the day at the hospital. Rhoda wondered anew about the wisdom of rehab for Ted and how soon they could all go home.

The Finks celebrated their twenty-sixth wedding anniversary three days later. Connie, the nurse, got flowers for Rhoda from Ted. Rhoda remained frustrated with Ted's lack of progress. "I'm not sure anybody knows what to do with Ted now," she wrote. "Personally, if he can get so he has his balance—can walk, eat a little, get to the bathroom—we're GONE!"

Blizzards and snow flurries now made the drives between Illinois and Wisconsin treacherous. Ted was showing enough progress that plans were being made to release him later in January, some fourteen months after he had first arrived on a stretcher. Rhoda bought him a La-Z-Boy chair and a new pair of eyeglasses, new shoes, and sweat pants. She continued to attend the burn-support group but with a new frame of mind, sensing that any meeting might be her last.

Rhoda was practically standing at the exit door, holding it open, but it did not appear that Ted would have the strength or breath to leave. His pain medications were leaving him groggy, and he had a disturbing shortness of breath. "I'm so sad that he isn't improving," Rhoda reflected. "Did we save him so he can't do a damn thing? That will be a good life for him."

After fifty-nine weeks Rhoda found herself despairing once more. "I worry a lot about everything. Chris says, 'Rehab. Rehab.' Ted says, 'Home. Home.' I say, 'Help. Help.' . . .

Ted not quite right, but I don't know why." On a Sunday in mid-January she thought that Ted seemed "groggy and loopy, and talks nonsense sometimes. Falls asleep in the middle of a sentence. . . . I don't know about going home. I'm not sure I can handle him. . . . All I want to do is cry. A real fun life.

"All my fears are coming true. Yep, Ted's OK, has skin, is alive. He can walk, but needs help. So he can't do anything for himself.

"What kind of life have I subjected him to? Hell on earth for the next 30 years? My life spent taking care of him? I had hoped and prayed for a better outcome. Let's be optimistic. Maybe everything will be better in what, 3-4-5 years?"

A few days later Ted was stronger. Rhoda could help him maneuver off the toilet, out of bed, out of a chair. He was able to get a burger and fries to his mouth on his own. With that feat, Rhoda told him, "I'm out half of a job." In the physical therapy gym he kept working on slow, clumsy steps. The hospital was growing more confident about Ted's release, and a date was scheduled in the coming few days. After dinner that night, Ted stopped and looked at himself for a time in the mirror. He kept gazing, angling his head, peering.

"He thinks he looks freaky," Rhoda wrote. "Well, I go with the fact that he looks different. But—I don't care. I think he looks good and I also think it will get better as we go. I know it's the worst for Ted to get used to. I feel bad for him and hope he'll be able to accept all of this. I pray it will get better for him."

Rhoda's diary entries consistently filled the whole page, top to bottom, every single day for more than a year. But not the entry for Saturday, January 20, 2001. In the middle of a blank page she wrote:

To apartment to pack and clean

No company

Ted just getting better

The following Tuesday, Chris drove up from Lanark to help carry Rhoda's belongings out of her apartment and to collect his father. When Rhoda finished getting her things into her car, she accidentally locked the keys inside. At noon the burn unit held a pizza party for Ted. At 1:30 in the afternoon, after 420 days in the hospital, Ted Fink was on his way home.

7

OLD SETTLERS

ᛒ THE FINK CLAN began calling Illinois home after the arrival, under questionable circumstances, of John Martin Fink. He emigrated from Stuttgart, in southern Germany, around the 1860s. It is not exactly clear why John Fink left Stuttgart, but he seemed to leave in a hurry, arriving with little more than a lengthy pipe with a cream-colored ceramic bowl that had two German words engraved on it: *Zum Andenken*, or loosely, "For Remembrance." Some Fink descendants believe their patriarch, a strapping young man when he made America his home, was trying to escape the military draft in Germany.

That was not the only murky issue surrounding the German immigrant. John M. Fink initially declared himself a blacksmith to census takers, but years later no Finks could recall his being anything but a farmer. He settled in northern Illinois because his sister, Anna, had already emigrated there herself. John settled first into the area of Logan County, in dead center of the long state. Three developers formed a new town there and gave it the surname of their bright young attorney, Abraham Lincoln. The tall angular lawyer christened the town of Lincoln himself, using the juice of a ripe watermelon. Lincoln rode his court circuit through Logan County and owned property there. Humble, Lincoln said when he christened the town that nothing named Lincoln had ever amounted to anything.

The fledgling railroad industry was helping to populate this prairie-turned-farmland. Irish immigrants built the railroads, and German immigrants worked in mines and on farms. Later the famed Route 66 would plow through both Logan County and Lincoln.

John Fink, the blacksmith-farmer, ended up working as a farmhand for a German-born widow, Catherine Dumpman Mertz. In something of a family scandal, he married the widow Mertz very soon after he began working on her farm. When Catherine took her new last name, Fink, she knew it was the German word for the small stout bird known as the finch. Finches have conelike bills that crush seeds. Some, like sparrows, are ground dwellers. Others, of various degrees of color, are tree dwellers. They do not migrate very far, preferring to stay close to home. Their fondness for weed seeds makes finches a favorite among farmers.

As the area in Illinois between Lake Michigan and the Mississippi River developed from prairie to organized settlement, a group from Maryland named the county after their fellow statesman, Charles Carroll, a signer of the Declaration of Independence.

Shortly before John Fink set foot on the dense soil of Carroll County, the state was organized into the township form of government. Carroll formed ten townships, some of their names reflecting the lingering attachments of pioneers to old haunts, in America, abroad, or in idealized visions: Freedom, Fairhaven, Lima, Shannon, Washington, Savanna, York, Woodland, and Salem. A small band of pioneers settled at the foot of a bluff to form what became Savanna. The name was appropriate since along the bluffs of the Mississippi, tall grass supplied forage for livestock.

Lanark was originally called Glasgow, but the name had to be changed in 1859 after it was discovered there was another Glasgow already in Illinois. It was then renamed to honor Lanark, Scotland, the hometown of immigrant bankers who funded the building of the Western Union railroad. The first house in Lanark, a sixteen-by-ninety-six-foot structure, was built as a boardinghouse for the men who were working on the railroad and also building a hotel called the Lanark House.

Basic supplies were scarce in Lanark, but the abundant land provided. In 1861, according to a journalist visiting from the London *Spectator*, "Indian corn, or corn as it is called here, is so plentiful that last winter it was burnt for fuel." Again, in the early 1870s, when corn prices dropped to a low of fifteen cents a bushel, farmers found it more economical to burn corn for fuel than to buy coal or even wood.

Lanark gradually became a busy shipping point. In 1877 area farmers shipped 379 carloads of grain and livestock east. Train wrecks were frequent. A big one occurred on September 9, 1884, just east of Lanark, according to the *Freeport Weekly Journal* (Faithful Herald of a Noisy World). The passengers walked into town to visit the locals. One Lanark man found himself talking to Chief Sitting Bull, the broken Sioux warrior, returning from Washington where he had just signed a pact with the government.

Around the time of Sitting Bull's appearance, John and Catherine Fink had their first child together, William. Three generations later his offspring would include Ted Fink. In all, John and Catherine had four children together. A boom had been under way for little Lanark, whose first store was a shop opened by "Uncle" Chancy Grant and his one-armed son, William. By 1878 there were seventy-five businesses, impressive for a town only twenty years old. Early industries included a sawmill, sash factory, woolen mill, gristmill, brickyards, creameries, cooper shop, marble works, carpet weavers, and boot and shoe makers, along with factories making corn plows, hand-powered washing machines, butter rubs, vinegar, corncob pipes, harnesses, and cheese. A small vegetable canning factory, which years later became Green Giant, packed peas, tomatoes, sweet corn, and pumpkin.

In 1888, a little before noon, the most destructive fire in Lanark history began, burning down four businesses and two buildings, a total loss of $50,000. Bucket brigades of citizens helped but could not contain the blaze to a single building, the Odd-Fellow's Hall. Five years later the Old School House was destroyed by fire early one Saturday morning when no students were around.

Many years later a Lanark historian, Caralee Aschen-brenner, vividly described her town: "Here are and have been all the elements which have made America: Indians, forts, wars, mineral lure, frontier life, settlements progressing to town by hardship and sacrifice, all done with a certain undramatic grace."

In Lanark and throughout Carroll County, older people, who longed for their bygone frontier days, formed Old Settler Societies. At club meetings they told and retold anecdotes from the early days, hoping to reconnect to a simpler, purer past. One Carroll County old-timer, quoted in the history book *Frontier Illinois*, recalled, "As the years increased, the productions of their farm and stock increased, and the memories of scanty meals and scanty wardrobes, physical hardships, etc., of their pioneer days were sweetened in the contemplation of farms and houses and barns and other surroundings of comfort their industry and perseverance had brought forth from the prairies and forests, that but a few years ago had been the grazing places of the buffalo, the elk and other animals natural to the wilds of the northwest, and the undisturbed hunting grounds of the red men.

"Although frontier Illinois faded, much remained the same. Households remained the basic social and economic block. . . . Residents tended gardens, raised poultry, and supplemented their diets with wild game, fish and wild berries and nuts. . . . Settlers from everywhere continued to use spinning wheels, hand looms and other traditional tools long after cheaper, mass-produced products rendered these tools unnecessary for all but the poorest folk. . . . People concerned themselves about friends, household members, church, school, work, and other personal facets of life."

Deeply nestled in Carroll County, the Finks were solid farm stock, adherents of the early-twentieth-century Prairie Farmer's Creed, which read in part:

I believe that the only good weed is a dead weed, and that a clean farm is as important as a clean conscience.

I believe in the farm boy and the farm girl, the farmer's best crops and the farmer's best hope.

I believe in the farm woman, and will do all in my power to make her life easier and happier.

I believe in community spirit, a pride in home and neighbors, and I will do my part to make my own community the best in the state.

I believe in happiness, I believe in the power of a smile, and I will use mine on every possible occasion.

I believe in the farmer, I believe in the farm life, I believe in the inspiration of the open country.

I am proud to be a farmer, and I will try earnestly to be worthy of the name.

In 1902 William Fink, first in the Fink family to be born a U.S. citizen, was twenty-six years old when he married twenty-one-year-old Wilhelmina Daehler. She went by the name Minnie, and her parents too had come from Germany. The two settled down on the family farm in Chadwick, a nearby town formed in 1886.

In 1904, the year of the St. Louis World's Fair (a few hours down the Mississippi), William and Minnie Fink had their first child, Elmer, who would become Ted Fink's grandfather. In Chadwick the Fink homestead, like many family farms of the time, needed all the hands it could raise. Shortly after Elmer was born, Carroll County's inhabitants included 41,648 cattle and 69,776 pigs, both of which easily outnumbered the human population of 18,035. On 1,822 farms, 543 farmers were native born and white, 278 were born abroad and white. The entire county had one black farmer.

Carroll County's productive soil churned out corn, oats, wheat, spelt (a variety of wheat), barley, buckwheat, rye, alfalfa, millet, potatoes, and yams; plums, prunes, apples, pears, peaches, nectarines, cherries, quinces, grapes, strawberries, raspberries, blackberries, loganberries, and dewberries.

Amid Lanark's thriving fields, one of the great scandals of the budding century happened on July 5, 1906. Ralph Whitmer, a boy of thirteen, climbed the hundred-foot steelwork of the Lanark water tower, opened a hole in its roof, took off his clothes, and dove in for a swim. He was discovered and arrested, and the tank was emptied out, scrubbed thoroughly, and pumped full of fresh water again. Still, many townspeople were indignant at the idea that they had to drink "bathwater."

Turn-of-the-century officials in Lanark could be sticklers. They once passed an ordinance outlawing the tossing of snowballs. And when one homeowner failed to pay for a city-sponsored sidewalk program, the town council paid workmen to rip up the sixty-foot sidewalk around his house and haul it away to the water works. The cement slabs were then installed around a firehouse.

At the time, the telephone was just beginning to change the nature of farming in remote communities. The Carroll County Independent Telephone Company began offering emergency toll line service, available exclusively to businesses and farmers eager for the latest market prices. The 1910 Lanark directory laid out some of the proper etiquette for the "telephonist." Sunday, for instance, was a day of rest. As there was only one operator on duty, a woman named Minta Swab, only business calls could be made before 7 p.m. And only extra-important calls were to be made after 10 p.m.

Farmers were also struggling to apply their skill to the contraption known as the motorcar. In 1917 the city council passed an ordinance that no fire "apparatus" could travel more than fifteen miles per hour in the city of Lanark. That followed an unfortunate mishap in which a gentleman named Harry Sites pulled a hose cart behind a Model T grocery truck and snapped a wheel off the truck.

Elmer Fink learned farming from his father and took a shine to a young woman named Cora Appel. She was a snappy dresser for a country woman at the time. She sat for a photo in the 1920s on the running board of a Model T sedan, her right leg crossed over her left, her skirt raised to reveal a good bit of stocking. She wore sleek high heels, an elegant wrap around her shoulders, and a stylish cloche, emblematic of the flapper era.

When Cora and Elmer were both twenty-one they sneaked away to Oregon, Illinois, a town forty-five miles from Chadwick, married in secret a week before Christmas, and returned—him to his parents' house, her to her parents' house—as if nothing had happened. Neither breathed a word about the marriage.

They eloped apparently to evade their parents' concerns about the young couple's plans to marry, though the Fink descendants remain unclear on just what the objections were. When the parents found out about the caper, they acquiesced and arranged for the couple to begin their marital life in a more normal fashion.

After high school, Elmer Fink taught in the public schools for a time, served as a justice of the peace, and took up farming full time. He was a religious man who served as Sunday school superintendent for a time in his Lutheran church in Chadwick. He died in 1948, leaving Cora, who had been raised by German farmers elsewhere in Carroll County, a widow at only forty-four. After Elmer's death the farm became her husband. She never remarried. She would go into the fields in her full-length skirt, feeding cattle and riding tractors, and supervising her two boys, Arnold, twenty-one then, and Vernon, seventeen.

Two years earlier Arnold had married June K. Miller, who was then eighteen. They had three children. In the early 1950s June laid her youngest, Ted, an infant boy, on a blanket in the yard just outside the house. In winter she wrapped him in a full-body snowsuit, his face peeking out from the furry hood. Around the time the boy turned three, when he could often be found playing with his toy tractor on the front porch, cancer was rapidly growing in his mother's uterus. When June Fink died at age twenty-nine, her three children were all still young. Judy Ann was ten, Gerald Fay was nine, and Ted was three.

June Fink died at home at 3:20 on a Tuesday morning in December 1957. At her funeral services the Reverend Paul Farley read selected scriptures and based his comforting remarks on Psalm 23, "The Lord is my shepherd; I shall not want . . ." A quartet of the young woman's friends sang, harmonizing on "In the Garden" and "When I Take My Vacation in Heaven."

Now a widower, Arnold Fink farmed his whole life in Chadwick and Lanark. He belonged to the Carroll County

Farm Bureau and superintended tractor pulls for the Carroll County Fair. It was not just the Finks who adored the fair. This was *the* great pastime in Carroll County in the 1950s and 1960s, attended by women in shirtwaist dresses and men in collared shirts, some wearing bow ties and panama hats. The 4-H Club king and queen—freckled teenagers in white floor-length gowns and black suits, ties, and corsages on lapels—were officially crowned.

Aside from being left with three small children when his wife died suddenly, Arnold Fink had duties at the fair and much work to do on the farm. He owed his house and the property he tilled to his mother, who, as a widow after Elmer was killed, got tough with equipment dealers and bankers. In the 1940s and 1950s they were not accustomed to doing business with women. Cora Fink was terse, direct, and opinionated. As the men dug ditches one day, Cora stood, hands on her hips, inspecting. She pointed out what they had done wrong and ordered them to redo it.

"Cora was either going to get tough or lose the farm," recalled Judy Fink, her granddaughter. So Cora rode the tractors theatrically in the field, her flapper dresses ruffling in the wind and her mud-caked boots firmly on the pedals. She could be a terror in a car. When she was out checking the progress of the corn one day, she veered into the wrong lane and ran a state policeman off the road. She then somehow talked her way out of a ticket. The story became part of Fink family lore, revived at reunions and holiday gatherings.

To the shame of some of the able-bodied men around Chadwick, Cora ran a highly successful cattle and grain operation and managed to put away enough cash to buy a farm in Lanark so that Arnold would have some land to work. In

March 1951 she paid $40,300 for the house and two hundred acres of prime soil.

Edward Dumroese was decidedly a city dweller when he arrived in America around 1879 from northern Germany. He settled into Chicago's West Side with many other immigrants and worked at some of the largest companies in that city of gleaming lights, including the McCormick Reaper Company (which later became International Harvester). He also worked at Western Electric, which made a fortune in the manufacture of fire alarms after the Great Chicago Fire of 1871 and later became the sole supplier of telephones to a country hungry for the newfangled devices. He and his wife, Louise, had seven children, including the middle child, Ernst.

Ernst Dumroese began dating Gertrude Kraft, a young woman who lived just around the corner from the Dumroese family, on Twenty-third Street. They were married in 1918. Ernst was exempt from service in World War I because of an eye condition. He did work evenings in the recruitment office, though, to help the armed forces. He was a studious man, and good with numbers. He became a bookkeeper at a business running greenhouses, then left to pursue a career as an independent accountant, mostly troubleshooting the shoddy work of other CPAs. He was not a certified public accountant himself and liked to joke that the abbreviation stood for Can't Prove Anything. He found himself on the road three weeks a month visiting with clients. The time away from his family was not working; something had to give.

So the Dumroese family moved in 1942 to Freeport, Illinois, about 115 miles west of Chicago. It put Ernst closer to his clients, who were spread throughout northern Illinois, and cut down his time on the road. Freeport was also friendly to Germans, who had moved from Pennsylvania in 1827 to begin settling in the Freeport area. One of them was William Baker, who built a trading post on the banks of the Pecatonica River and became well known for his altruism. He began operating a free ferry to transport people across the river and often invited visitors into his home for lodging.

The Dumroese family's move from Chicago put them in touch with a long-standing Freeport family, the Kastens. LeeRoy Wilhelm Kasten co-owned the Superior Dairy in Freeport, and Ernst Dumroese came one day to do his books. Lee was viewed in his family as a force to be reckoned with, ever since a mentally deranged man had viciously attacked him with a cane.

Through the contact, Ronald Dumroese, Ernst's son, acquired a milk-delivery route. But Ronald Dumroese got more than a job from old man Kasten: he began dating his daughter, Janet Lee, and by the time she was twenty-one, they were married. The couple worked hard, Ronald for years as a meter reader for the gas company. They had a modest house in the center of town. Ronald could not serve in the army because of a detached retina. Janet had worked since she was fourteen, first at a battery company, and then, during her marriage, as a bailiff at the courthouse and in data processing for a company that later became part of Honeywell.

Life at the Dumroese house revolved around the church. There were always fund-raisers, chili suppers, and basketball games to attend. The Immanuel Lutheran Church, on East Pleasant Street, was a large brick building with a soaring steeple topped with a cross. Built in 1900 at a cost of $13,000, the church would mark life passages for generations of Dumroese family members. Janet and Ronald had three children. The middle one, a girl, was born on October 4, 1953. They named her Rhoda.

8

GETTING BY

♞ BY THE TIME Ted and Rhoda left the hospital, Ted's case, No. 165-12-50, filled twenty accordion files of charts and medical notes, each nearly two inches thick. End to end the stack of paper records stood three feet tall.

In Lanark the Dumroese and Fink families descended on the farmhouse where Ted had grown up to welcome him home and to help Rhoda. Judy was on hand. Rhoda's mother, Janet, came in from Freeport. Chris and Deanna helped. "I was so weak when I came home that I couldn't open the car door," Ted recalled.

Homecoming was Tuesday, January 23, 2001. On that first day back, Ted asked Chris to help him up onto his re-furbished John Deere 610C Turbo—the same tractor he had been driving when the accident happened. "First thing he needed to do when he got back," Chris recalled. Ted sat on Chris's shoulder, and his hulking son pushed him up into the little glassed-in cabin. Repairing the tractor after the fire had cost fourteen thousand dollars.

"You got to get at peace with yourself for whatever happened," Ted explained later, recalling that day. "You have this fear—I don't want to be around that stuff anymore. The goal in getting back on the tractor was to live life not afraid of things. So I decided I either get back with it right away, or forget it."

He stayed on it only about twenty minutes. He was too tired for more. "I didn't have the gas. Nevertheless I got over a hurdle."

That night Ted and Rhoda were exhausted. Rhoda slept in their bed, Ted in a hospital bed they had bought for his return home. Ted was restless, getting up twice during the night, and Rhoda ended up listening to his strained breathing throughout the night.

Four days into their homecoming it was Ted's forty-seventh birthday. Rhoda's mother and Judy each brought a cake. They all sang "Happy Birthday." The cakes had no flickering candles.

An ice storm the following Sunday night knocked out the electricity at home through Monday morning, preventing Ted and Rhoda from returning for scheduled appointments in Madison. Although he was home, Ted faced follow-up visits in the burn clinic to ensure he was healing properly and would not need to be readmitted. Rhoda did not know what she would do with herself if Ted had to go back in the hospital. With Rhoda's help, Ted could get in and out of their car, a blue Dodge Caravan, for the drive to Madison.

The first checkup went well. Ted's skin was healing properly, and his vital signs looked positive. Rhoda was relieved, particularly because he had been sleeping for hours on end when he returned home. She worried that he would slip into decline again and that more time in Madison was inevitable.

She appreciated small steps. She had developed a reliable system for bathing Ted and changing his dressings. First, she would help him into their tiny bathroom. She would undress him and cut all the bandages off his torso, legs, and behind. Then she would help him into the shower. As he stood there, covered with sores, she would rinse him with a hand-held showerhead, gently scrub him with soap, and rinse him again. Then she would apply lotion to his skin.

She would clean the small device inserted in his throat in case he needed to be hooked up to a breathing machine again. Then she would wrap him in fresh bandages called pressure garments. They were made of woven fabric similar to support hose. The garments were difficult to fasten, and they had to fit very tight as they were designed to smooth out the skin surface and reduce scarring. They had zippers on the sides, and Rhoda fought to zip them over Ted's legs, arms, and hands. She ordered the medical garments in green and yellow, the colors of his John Deere equipment. The entire process took three hours. "You end up planning your life around his bath," she said one day.

On a grey Monday in February after Ted's return home, Rhoda was doing laundry when the phone rang. It was an investigator for the Carnegie Hero Fund, the group that was considering awards to the two neighbors who had put out the flames engulfing Ted on the afternoon of his accident. She spoke with the man for some time.

Rhoda had just about given up her diary at this point, going days with no entries, and on this particular day she wrote little beyond "Dreary day. Ted sleeps a lot."

The Saturday before Valentine's Day, Rhoda's mother visited again from Freeport, and the mother and daughter made heart-shaped cookies. Ted had virtually returned to a comatose state. The least activity exhausted him. Once home, he began to recognize his new limitations. "When I came home, I had pretty much given up," he recalled. "I could barely walk."

He went with Rhoda to the burn clinic the following Monday, and the decision was made not to remove the plug in his throat. Ted was no longer using a breathing machine, but doctors decided for precautionary reasons to have him ready to hook up to a ventilator at a moment's notice. Rhoda was disappointed but felt the visit was otherwise promising.

Privately, Dr. Schurr was stunned. Fully fourteen months after the accident, after he had leaned over the operating table applying Ted's artificial skin and patching his patient back together piece by piece, Dr. Schurr could not believe how weak Ted looked and how little physical ability he had regained. "To put it bluntly, I'd see Ted in the clinic early on," Dr. Schurr recalled, "and I'd think to myself: I made the wrong decision."

Snow showers arrived two days later, and at 6:30 in the morning Rhoda awoke at the sound of a horrible thud. Ted had fallen out of bed. "Scares me to death," she wrote in her diary. She called for Chris to come hoist his dad back into bed. Ted had a fat lip and was coughing up blood. It was Valentine's Day.

That night Rhoda wrote in her diary, "I'm pretty much shot here emotionally. I've spent the day crying. Crying for Ted, me, what we've lost and probably won't ever get back. . . . I feel so empty inside. I'm giving, giving, and not getting any love back." Then she added, "But it's not about me—it's about Ted."

March came in on pins and needles. For reasons that puzzled his doctors, Ted began feeling buzzing sensations all over his body. It was the kind of fuzzy tingling that follows a bump on the funny bone. "I was just pins and needles throughout my body—it was like an arm waking up from falling asleep, but everywhere," Ted said. He went to a rehabilitation clinic in Rockford, closer than Madison but still an hour's drive away. Taking steps as he held parallel bars or a helper's arm, he was still basically toddling. "It took months to take that first step. I fell down a lot," he recalled.

In the weeks that followed, Ted tried to relearn such things as brushing his teeth and holding a fork. Rhoda drove him back and forth to rehab. She dressed him. She fed him. She brushed his teeth. Rehab workers tried to limber up his arms and legs.

Therapists measure "degrees of movement" in determining stages of disability and improvement. With his rigid joints, Ted had measurements that were quite poor. "First year we were home, I didn't do anything," he recalled. By the second summer he was able to maneuver into his minivan. With adaptive devices to help him turn the key in the ignition and turn the steering wheel, he could drive into the fields to watch the boys and the progress of the crops.

Some days he resisted going to rehabilitation. He found it exhausting and not all that helpful. Rhoda persisted. "I told

Ted, 'Your New Year's resolution is to brush your own teeth—I'm giving up the job.'" With help from the therapists, Ted improved his degrees of movement in one elbow just enough to do it himself.

Just weeks before Ted's accident, Chris had applied to attend the University of Wisconsin in Platteville, where he had planned to study agricultural engineering. His dream was to work for John Deere in equipment design. As a boy he had loved farm machinery, and in his late teens and early twenties he had taken what money he could earn to buy antique combines and tractors. He was particularly proud of his John Deere No. 55 model combine, one of the company's first self-propelled models.

Deere, whose worldwide headquarters were in downstate Moline, beckoned. "I thought it'd be fun to test out the new prototype equipment," he said. But that was all put on hold after his father landed in the hospital and just stayed there month after month. Chris kept putting off his registration. "At the college they were real nice about it after dad's accident. They gave me an extension for enrolling," he recalled. "I had even picked out a dorm room."

At the same time Chris began getting serious about his girlfriend. He had met Deanna when they were attending Highland Community College, just outside Freeport. She would ride with him to see his father in Madison and keep him company when Rhoda was away on weekdays.

Chris had learned a lot from his father about working the soil, but he had not been paying the kind of attention one pays if he thinks he may suddenly have to do it all himself. He ran the farm in the months while Ted was comatose, with

only minor mistakes. After he awoke, though still hospital-
ized, Ted recalled how he "was trying to run the grain dryer
from the hospital bed. I was taking calls from Chris on the
cell phone. The burner was not up to temperature; he could
not get the burner hot enough. I had him open the valve on
the propane. We got her going."

In late 1999 Peter had been away at college in Ashland,
Ohio, where he was studying computers. When he heard
about the accident on that grim Saturday night in November,
he and a friend drove through the night, reaching Madison at
5 a.m. After seeing the severity of his father's condition, he decided not to go back to school during the next growing season, to help mind the family business instead. No one asked
him to. "It's just a thing you had to do," he later recalled.
"When the family farm is your livelihood, it has to go on."

Having spent his whole life in Carroll County, and having
been blessed with an inborn compass, Ted knew his way
around these parts perfectly. He was a trusty guide, never lost.
He would find his way from town or the fields or the quarries back to the driveway, off Maple Grove Road to the two-
story white farmhouse—as if on automatic pilot. He drove
several cars after the blue Nova, but none was as special as his
black 1947 Pontiac Streamliner two-door coupe. The massive
car, a rolling monument to chrome and steel, had belonged
to one of the Finks' landlords in Lanark, Bill Bright. Ted had
looked longingly at it for years, asking repeatedly to buy it.

In the fall of 1997 Bright gave in, parting with the curvy
old automobile for five hundred dollars. It had been sitting in

one of his sheds, with a dirt floor, since 1961. Ted was only
the Streamliner's second owner, and it had just thirty thousand miles on it. The body was in good shape, with no rust,
and the hubcaps, chrome strips, and hood ornament were intact. The interior had been damaged by mildew and mice. Ted
began restoring it in January 1998. He worked on it with Peter and Chris, who were intrigued by this antique. The lug
nuts on the left side of the car tightened by turning left, or
counterclockwise, while the ones on the right tightened to
the right. The car had a floor starter button, which could
make ignition tricky. You had to push in the clutch with the
left foot and use the right foot for the starter. It had a manual shift and no power brakes or steering. The windshield
washers were fed from a fruit jar screwed on under the hood.
The way the wipers ran off the engine, they would slow almost to a stop when you accelerated up a hill, but then would
speed up on the downhill ride.

Over several months Ted restored much of the car,
adding fat new tires, brake lines, a new fuel pump, and a fresh
coat of black paint on the exterior. He and the boys fixed all
the dashboard instruments, including the clock, and delicately
repainted the dial needles. The bumpers and chrome from inside the car were sent to Chicago for refurbishing. Ted had a
cousin in nearby Milledgeville who owned The Chevy Shop.
He helped with the chrome and with finding the proper
paint so as to keep everything authentic. The engine, a blocky
eight-cylinder job, needed no repair. Under the hood, all they
did was to replace some hoses and belts.

The upholstery was a mess, with mildew, rot, and mouse
nests. The Finks took the seats to Clinton, Iowa, and had
them redone by a shop there. The original seats were made of

grey wool, and they replaced them with a grey and burgundy stripe.

By the time the Streamliner was spiffed up, it was the summer of 1999, and Ted and Rhoda drove it to Freeport several times. They took it all around Lanark and drove it to church and to the bank in Chadwick. "It was always quite the conversation piece when we were out and about," Rhoda recalled. Chris took Deanna on dates in the old car.

Ted proudly parked it outside the house he had grown up in. Arnold Fink had moved into the house in 1951 from Chadwick, a few minutes' drive southwest. When Arnold arrived with June and his two young children, the house had no electricity. The farmhouse had been built in 1870; the floor beams still had bark on them when Cora Fink bought the place. When Arnold and his family moved in there were potbellied stoves to heat each side of the house. Arnold installed the bathroom.

The house was a sturdy, reliable structure for Ted and Rhoda and their boys, and it was the repose Ted sought at the end of every day. It had a small but functional kitchen as well as a little living room and a utility room for the washer and dryer on the ground floor, and three bedrooms on the second floor.

When they returned from the hospital, though, Ted and Rhoda quickly found that their longtime house had flaws. It was hard each night for Ted to get up and down the creaky stairs to get to bed. The bathroom was small, which made it difficult for Ted and Rhoda to maneuver as she helped bathe him.

When Chris and Deanna became engaged, Ted and Rhoda decided the old farmhouse would no longer work for the family. After the hospital charges and Rhoda's expenses in living out of apartments and suitcases for a year, they did not have much left for a down payment on a new house, so they decided to buy a less expensive manufactured home. It was mid-August 2001 when they contacted Wick Building Systems of Mazomanie, Wisconsin. The Finks ordered the Cardinal Creek model, an eighteen-hundred-square-foot house, including basement. "We couldn't afford a stick-built one," recalled Ted. Compared with their old home, the new one had wider doors, a handicapped-accessible bathroom in the master bedroom, and, mercifully, no steps in and out of any doors. "It was handier for Ted," said Rhoda, "with no steps."

The foundation work for the basement was completed before Thanksgiving, two years after Ted's accident, and the new house arrived on two trailers in early December. The flooring came in sections; the outside walls and the trusses were prebuilt. Within days the workmen pieced together the place, which was L-shaped with a two-car garage that jutted out in front. The other leg of the structure—the front door and the living space—was parallel to Maple Grove Road. The new house, whose exterior was the color of butter, was located a stone's throw from the old one, which was to become Chris and Deanna's home after their marriage.

On New Year's Day 2002, the Finks were preparing for the move when Rhoda picked up her diary for the first time in months. "As you can see," she wrote, "I kind of gave up on the journal last February. No time to write! Looking back I can see how things have improved for Ted, therefore for me. He can now feed himself, take his own medications, walk by himself—in and out of the chair—bed—helps with the laundry."

Ted and Rhoda moved in February. Inside the new front doorway, Rhoda placed a framed cross-stitching that had been in the family for ages. In embroidered Gothic lettering it said: *Lobe den Herrn, meine Seele.* It was Psalm 103:1 in German, meaning, "Bless the Lord, my soul."

On Easter Sunday Ted awoke in the new house at three in the morning to use the bathroom and found blood everywhere in the bed. His skin was still healing on his legs and his backside, and occasionally, with diminished feeling, he was not aware that he was bleeding. Pressuring the wounds, Rhoda stopped the flow of blood. It is normal, as part of the body's healing process, for wounds to try to close up, to contract, and surgeons can alleviate some of this shrinkage by doing a procedure called a "release." In that operation they typically cut out the hardened scar tissue and replace it with a skin graft. Patients find it enormously painful because the surgeons must slice off healthy skin from elsewhere on their body to donate to the site of the old scar. And sometimes, after all the trouble, the spot simply fails to heal well enough to be as flexible as hoped.

That summer Ted had a neck release procedure done and two such operations on his belly. And he continued to go to physical therapy, often for four hours a day. It was all for good cause. He wanted to attend Chris's wedding, set for the summer of 2002. He needed to keep his strength up and work to become more limber so he could get into the church and out as independently, and inconspicuously, as possible. That June, Chris and Deanna were married at the First Lutheran Church in Chadwick, where Chris and his older brother had been baptized years before.

The story is told that Henry Ford was partly motivated to invent the automobile because, as a boy on a farm in Michigan, he experienced the loneliness of rural life, with neighbors remote, living miles and miles apart. Ted Fink faced the same fate if he had not had his minivan adapted for his crippled hands, and if he could not maneuver himself well enough to get into the driver's seat. The Dodge Caravan, with its handicapped license plates, offered a dose of freedom to Ted's new life of limits. He could pull up to the garage that jutted out in front of the house, and with the flip of a switch raise the door. "Garage-door opener is a wonderful thing," he said one day.

But he had to make adjustments. That summer he found he had to roll the windows up instead of enjoying the warm air blasting his face as the van hurtled down the road. The bows of his black-frame glasses were resting on ear-lobe stumps, since most of his external ear structure was burned off. "When you don't have ears," he explained, "the wind just howls—it's fiercely loud."

And for some reason that his doctors couldn't explain, Ted found that after the accident he had lost his good sense of direction. For the first time in his life he was having difficulty finding his way around his community. He began repeating little mantras that helped reset his internal compass: east-west route numbers are even; north-south ones are odd.

Some in the community found it difficult to adjust to the new Ted. His skin had turned tough and crusty in spots; his coloration was a patchwork of bone-white, peach, and blush-red. Going out in public was challenging. "Some people act like they used to act," Ted said. Others stared or turned away. "Some people flat-ass ignore you. You find out who your friends are." He added, "I know I don't look very good."

One day in March 2003, Ted pulled into the driveway, got out of the Caravan, and began walking toward the garage. He slipped, and tumbled down. His arms and legs were so bent and rigid that he could not get himself up on his feet. He was immobile, a turtle on its back. He shouted and called, but Rhoda and Deanna, who was expecting then, were in the house talking and didn't hear him. Eventually he just closed his eyes and rested there. They did not find him until sometime later.

9

HEROIC MEASURES

✻ THE LETTER that came to the sixteenth floor of the old Alcoa Building, on Sixth Avenue in downtown Pittsburgh, was extravagant in its praise. "In over 20 years of involvement with Emergency Medical Services, this is by far the most self-less act of civilian heroism I have ever witnessed," it began. It was from Dr. Michael Abernathy, medical director of Lifeline Helicopter at St. Anthony Medical Center in Rockford, Illinois. He was recommending Mark and Duane Plock, the two neighbors who had rescued Ted Fink from the field of fire, for a Carnegie Hero Award.

Each year accounts of eight hundred to a thousand rescues in the United States and Canada are submitted to the Carnegie Hero Fund Commission in Pittsburgh. A handful of investigators there review them, verify the details of the events, and ultimately decide whether each rescue is indeed heroic. Some are easy calls. In 1996 Lora K. Drake, a twenty-one-year-old from Indianapolis, was driving by a pasture in Illinois when she saw a 950-pound bull mauling a woman. She stopped, climbed through an electric fence, and began striking the bull with a two-foot length of rubber tubing until the victim could escape.

The commission, which administers the award dreamed up by the industrialist Andrew Carnegie in 1904, has classified heroic acts into those involving fire, water, suffocation, electric shock, moving vehicles, high elevation, homicidal attack, and aggression by enraged animals.

Only about 11 percent of the rescue accounts hold up to the Carnegie tests for a true hero. The number of medalists varies each year. Winners receive a bronze medal, a $3,500 cash award and, occasionally, a scholarship or pension. Most of the cases come to the commission through a clipping service that scans newspapers and other media for accounts of heroism. It also accepts nominations.

The commission's rules may seem stringent, perhaps even unfair, but they are as tough as the people they recognize. Police and firefighters are ineligible except in extreme circumstances: their jobs call for putting their lives on the line. Rescuing a family member typically is not deemed heroic either, unless the rescuer loses his or her life or is severely injured. According to the rules, "Members of the armed forces and children considered by the commission to be too young to comprehend the risks involved are also ineligible for consideration."

To qualify, a person must be a civilian who voluntarily risks his or her life to an extraordinary degree trying to save the life of another person. So Larry Champagne, an eleven-year-old St. Louis boy who made headlines in the mid-1990s for bringing a runaway school bus with other children aboard to a stop on a busy highway, would not qualify. He was saving his own life too. Walter F. Rutkowski, the Hero Fund's executive director, says the commission received one application from a man filing on behalf of his wife. "He was retired military. She was pushing a baby stroller across the street when a car suddenly turned the corner and struck her. She, allegedly, pushed the stroller out of the way at the last moment and saved the baby."

A sure act of heroism? Not to the Carnegie Hero Fund Commission. "Doesn't count," Rutkowski said, sitting perfectly upright in a dark suit and tie in his corner office at the Alcoa Building. "She just happened to be in the path of the car. She did not voluntarily put herself in danger to save someone else. The woman was in a coma when her husband wrote. He wrote a strong protest after the award was denied."

The commission goes to great lengths to corroborate the exact details of any given incident, partly to establish the motives of the rescuer, partly to sift out hoaxes, and partly to divide phenomenal acts of self-sacrifice from exaggerated claims of selflessness. One locally publicized water rescue fell apart after the commission's investigators discovered that the schoolchildren who claimed to be heroes actually made the whole story up as a cover for playing hooky.

Commission investigators take nothing for granted. They interview witnesses. They check police and hospital records. They question. They doubt. They often refer to their well-thumbed "Manual of Instructions for Field Representatives." Under the heading "Attack by a Horned Animal," for instance, investigators learn that they are required to report the precise spread of the antlers as well as the number of prongs and their average length.

Edward Harper, a thirty-five-year-old insurance salesman, jumped into a deep, icy stream at a park one Sunday in

Youngstown, Ohio, to save a youngster who had fallen in. He won a Carnegie award, but not before being grilled by investigators. The inquiry, he told a newspaper, "seemed to go almost to the point of ridiculousness. They wanted to know the distances, depths, temperatures, speeds of the stream."

Investigators work hard to reward the truly worthy and to protect the award's integrity. "There was one woman who the papers said ran into a burning house to save some neighbor children," said Rutkowski. She applied for the award. In checking official accounts, investigators quickly found troubling discrepancies. "Her own statement to the fire department and the fire marshal is that she stood outside the house and helped the children out through the window." Her nomination was denied. Official documents, usually written up hours after the rescue, have been especially valuable to the commission. "The farther you get from an act of heroism," said Rutkowski, "the braver the hero."

Would the nominees in the rescue of Ted Fink hold up to the commission's scrutiny? The Plock brothers' actions appeared commendable, at least according to the account of Dr. Abernathy, the emergency helicopter physician who brought the actions of the men to the attention of the commission. He described how the men selflessly ran to the cornfield to find Ted Fink who was caught in a fire. The accident involved a fire, a propane tank, and a man saved. All looked promising.

When the commission decided to look into the rescue of the Illinois farmer, the case of Duane and Mark Plock became the 74,455th and 74,456th claims to be investigated by the commission. Among the hundreds of cases it considered that year, 2001, a few stand out. In Reserve, Louisiana, one-year-old Jeremy Posey was left onboard a seventeen-foot motorboat one afternoon in July 2000 after his parents fell overboard. The boat sped along out of control but in tight circles on Lake Maurepas. A man in another boat tried to stop the circling boat, but his boat overturned when the two vessels collided. Darkness fell as the circling boat remained out of control for more than thirty minutes, with marine patrollers and other rescuers responding to the scene. Then thirty-three-year-old Guy Adams, a state wildlife agent, and a partner approached the baby's boat in their own twenty-one-foot vessel. As his partner steered their boat into the path of the runaway, Adams leaped from the bow of their boat into the back of the fugitive craft and pulled the throttle, stalling the motor. The baby onboard was unharmed.

In Port Alice, British Columbia, Jon M. Nostdal was riding his bicycle on an unlit road one night in February 2001 when a cougar leaped from behind him onto his back, pulled the fifty-two-year-old man from the roadway, and began to maul him. He fought against the cougar for several minutes as it bit his arms and head. Elliot Ralph Cole, a thirty-nine-year-old instrument mechanic, was driving by in his truck when he spotted the brawl. Pulling over, he searched for some sort of weapon to fend off the cougar. He finally grabbed a gym bag filled with books and began slugging the animal. Failing, he began pounding the cougar with his fists. It would not release Nostdal. Cole then picked up Nostdal's bicycle and attacked the cougar with it. The cougar released his prey but kept Nostdal's jacket in its jaws. Nostdal slipped out of the jacket, and the two men dashed for the truck, slammed the doors, and drove off. At the hospital, Nostdal required sutures for numerous puncture wounds and lacerations.

In Bellingham, Washington, seventy-year-old Herbert Bepler was rolling along in his motorized wheelchair when it became lodged at a crossing next to a railroad track. A train was approaching at about thirty miles per hour. Minutes earlier, Wade Handsaker, an eighteen-year-old college student, had bicycled past and saw Bepler near the track before his wheelchair became trapped. Aware the train was approaching, he sensed he ought to return to the crossing. He saw Bepler's wheelchair stuck. As the train bore down, Handsaker struggled to dislodge the wheelchair. A projection of the locomotive struck Bepler and severed his lower left leg. He was treated at a hospital, underwent rehabilitation, and recovered.

In South Lake Tahoe, California, Steven Maclean, a fifty-one-year-old truck driver, lost consciousness in the morning rush hour while driving his tractor-trailer along an interstate highway one day in August 2000. The rig left the highway and, traveling along at twenty-five miles per hour, hit a concrete side wall and continued along the shoulder. It was headed for the ramps of a busy highway interchange just a half-mile away. At its rate of speed, the runaway truck would enter the path of morning commuters in a little more than a minute.

Spotting the truck, Jeffrey Gartner, a twenty-eight-year-old highway patrolman on duty that morning, drove up alongside, and, peering in the driver's side window, saw the driver slumped over in his seat. Gartner had an idea, but it would require split-second timing. He raced ahead of the truck, pulled over onto the shoulder, and ran toward the approaching tractor-trailer, which had now slowed to about fifteen miles per hour. He jumped onto the running board of the tractor, opened the driver's door, and mashed the brake pedal, halting the vehicle just before it would have hit his squad car. Gartner and another passerby removed the immobile driver from the truck and worked to revive him until other help arrived. The man was taken to the hospital but died two days after he suffered the heart attack that put him in his behind-the-wheel predicament.

In late July 2000, as he drove across a bridge in Akron, Ohio, Gene Barker, a fifty-nine-year-old retired mason, saw a woman sitting on a narrow concrete barrier along the edge of a highway bridge, a point seventy feet above a paved road. After passing her, he returned, parked his car a distance away, and then slowly approached on foot. He spoke to her for several minutes. The woman told him she was going to jump, and she braced to leap. Barker lunged at her from about four feet away and grasped her in his arms. They tussled, Barker leaning over the waist-high barrier and the woman screaming at him to let go. Other men who happened by helped Barker hold the woman until emergency crews arrived and took her from the bridge to the hospital.

In late December 1999, Rosanne Coleman found her life endangered when a car accident sent her sport utility vehicle off the highway in Brighton, Ontario. It came to rest on a railroad track. The woman, who was twenty-six, lay unconscious at the edge of the track, next to her vehicle. Ross Chalmers, a fifty-seven-year-old petroleum marketer, stopped along with other motorists, seeing the overturned vehicle. They spied a train approaching at fifty miles per hour. Chalmers and another man immediately grabbed the woman and pulled her from danger. They were only twenty feet away when the train, its emergency brakes squealing, struck the

SUV, scattering debris. In the collision, the vehicle shot forward fifty feet. Coleman recovered.

These were the official summaries by the investigative staff of the Carnegie Hero Fund, which awarded each of the rescuers a medal. There is no awards ceremony; the medals are simply mailed. In all, there have been a dozen Carnegie Hero Funds around the world. Only the German branch, established in 1911, the *Carnegie-Stiftung für Lebensretter*, closed. It went belly up during the reign of the Third Reich.

The youngest Carnegie hero ever was a seven-year-old girl in Manitowoc, Wisconsin, who died after saving her brother from a fire in their home in 1995. The eldest was an eighty-six-year-old woman in Hueytown, Alabama, who tried to save her invalid son from a fire in his home in 2002. Roughly 20 percent of the hero medals have been awarded posthumously. Most rescues involved fire and water. In its first century, the fund gave away about $28 million.

Each Carnegie medal is a round bronze medallion, the size of a coffee coaster, with Andrew Carnegie's embossed profile on the front. On the other side are sprigs of laurel, representing glory; ivy, for friendship; oak, for strength; and thistle, for persistence. The leaves and branches adorn the cartouche, or small engraved tablet, which identifies the hero by name and briefly explains the deed. Around the outer edge, encircling the leaves and branches, is a quotation from John 15:13: "Greater love hath no man than this, that a man lay down his life for his friends."

Andrew Carnegie, the great steel magnate and philanthropist, was moved to establish the award to recognize society's heroes after a massive coal-mining explosion in 1904 in Harwick, a tiny community along the Allegheny River, north of Pittsburgh. The accident claimed some 181 lives and led Carnegie to issue gold medals to two rescuers who died in the mines trying to save others—strangers. He looked into the financial wherewithal of the men's surviving families. He penciled a note, "I can't get those widows and children of the mine out of my head." Two months later he drafted a deed to establish the Hero Fund, setting aside an endowment of $5 million.

"We live in an heroic age," he wrote in the founding papers, which are framed in the commission's offices. "Not seldom are we thrilled by the deeds of heroism where men or women are injured or lose their lives in attempting to preserve or rescue their fellows."

Looking further into the claims of Dr. Abernathy, Carnegie investigators found that Ted Fink had been in his tractor, hauling a propane tank, which having been accidentally dropped, suddenly had a leak. "Instead of air, the engine was now breathing propane gas," Dr. Abernathy wrote in his initial letter to the Hero Fund. "Ted, aware of the danger, quickly shut off the key and jumped from the tractor. Within a few seconds, the tractor backfired. The whole area erupted into a fireball 300 feet in diameter, consuming Ted, his tractor, and the 3/4-full propane tank."

Describing the deeds of the rescuers, he added, "Approximately 70 feet into the fireball, Mark [Plock] stumbled onto what he thought was a burning pile of old rubble or an old tire—it was Ted." The first fire department truck arrived on the scene seven to ten minutes after the 911 call was placed. "An eternity in hell," were the words Duane Plock used to describe it, Dr. Abernathy recalled in his letter. As Ted was taken away by ambulance, Dr. Abernathy wrote, the Plock brothers "sat there, their coveralls and hair still smoldering."

The Carnegie investigators wrote to the Plock brothers, asking for their own detailed accounts of the incident. Mark Plock's report was straightforward. He and his son were hauling corn near the Fink farm on the afternoon of the accident when they heard the explosion and spotted Ted and his tractor.

"Everything was burning," wrote Mark Plock, a burly thirty-nine-year-old farmer who was six feet tall and 220 pounds, basically Ted's build. He wore coveralls and a cap that day. The fire roared, fed by the propane gas and hovering a few feet above the ground, leaving some room for him to crawl below it, like a soldier bellying along.

"I ran to the tractor and Ted wasn't inside. I started to yell his name, and heard a moan. I could see what I thought was a pile of cornstalks burning and realized it was Ted. Tried to put him out with my hands, but couldn't. I crawled up and laid right on top of him to smother out the fire.

"I put my hands on his head to put out the fire there. I got off of him and was kneeling alongside of him when a low pocket of liquid petroleum exploded directly behind me and blew me back on top of him."

Duane, his forty-two-year-old brother, was about a mile away when he heard the explosion and raced over. He was a farmer and carpenter. The two worked in concert amid the flames to save Ted. Mark told the investigators, "I got off him again and he just ignited again. So after a couple of times of trying to keep him from igniting, we put him out with dirt, which worked. I covered his face with my hat to keep the smoke and flames off his face. We then cut off all the smoldering clothes that were left on him."

Duane's report was similar. He concluded it by writing: "My brother is also sending you his account. I hope this is what you want. It was the longest and shortest 15 minutes of our lives."

The investigators interviewed Rhoda. Some of her remarks were striking, coming from the wife of the victim. "Ted was on the ground, clothes burning, eyeglasses burning on his face. . . . It was 40 degrees that day, no wind. . . . It took the firefighters less than 10 minutes to arrive—a real miracle because they [were] seven miles away. . . . It's an all-volunteer fire station . . . but all the firemen were there playing cards, waiting for their wives to come back from their Christmas shopping."

In his report of his interview with Rhoda, one investigator wrote, "She wouldn't call the Plocks 'friends' but they were well acquainted as lifelong neighbors." A closer relationship could have posed a problem for the judges at the Hero Fund. Rhoda's interviewer found her to be "honest and credible."

Still, commission investigators wanted more. They requested hospital records to corroborate the claims that the Plocks suffered minor burns. In time they checked out. But the investigators wanted still more. They interviewed the local fire chief, and Mark Plock's son who was with his father when the fire broke out, and another neighbor who responded to the scene. They also reviewed the state fire marshal's report of the accident.

Once all the i's were dotted and the t's crossed, investigator Paul Snatchko filed an official account for the board of the commission to judge whether they had heroes on their hands or not.

ACCIDENT:

Ted A. Fink was at his farm moving a 1,000-gallon tank that held about 100 gallons of propane, a flammable gas stored under pressure as liquid. The cylindrical tank was about 16 feet long and 3.4 feet in diameter, and it had a valve on its underside. Fink had attached the tank by chains to a loader bucket at the front of the tractor and was intending to relocate it from near his house to a point outside of a barn.

The house and barn were near the entrance to the 200-acre farm, as were grain bins, a machine shop, a machine shed, and two other tanks containing liquid propane, each of 8,000-gallon capacity. Inside the house was Fink's wife, 46. Air temperature outside was about 40 degrees; there was no wind. It was becoming dark.

When Fink had reached a point near the barn, one of the chains broke and one end of the tank fell and struck the ground. The tank was damaged and began to leak. Fink re-attached the tank to the tractor, and, to get it away from the farm structures, took it west into a harvested cornfield. To do so, he drove the tractor in reverse and dragged the tank. After going about 360 feet, or when he reached a point about 50 feet into the field that was west of the machine shed, Fink detached the tank, then started to drive the tractor away.

Consensus of testimony was that propane vapor penetrated the tractor's engine, which began to accelerate. The engine backfired, and the propane vapor ignited explosively into a cloud of fire that was described as about 200 feet wide and 50 feet high. Stubble in the immediate area began to burn, the ground fire eventually encompassing about three acres. Propane that continued to escape from the tank, which remained intact, also ignited. Fink came to lie supine on the ground west of the tractor, about 15 feet southwest of the tank. He was engulfed by fire, his clothes and eyeglasses burning.

Mark Steven Plock and his son, 15, at a farm about an eighth-mile to the north, had seen Fink move the tank and subsequent events. After the propane ignited, Mark ran to his truck and sped to the scene as his son went to the farmhouse to call 911. Fink's wife, meanwhile, had heard the propane ignite; she then saw the fire cloud and also called 911. From the farm directly east of Fink's, Mark's brother, Duane, also witnessed the accident, and he too immediately drove to the scene, over a course about a mile in length. As Mark drove to Fink's farm, he later stated, he smelled a strong scent of propane. Later, stating that he did not want his truck to blow up, Mark . . . exited the vehicle at the south end of the shed. He proceeded on foot to the burning field, where, he later stated, 'everything was burning.'

The initial large fire cloud had burned away after a few minutes, but some vapors remained burning, starting at a point three feet above the ground. The chief of the responding fire department later stated that the concentration of vapor had been so thick near the ground that it could not burn there. Also, flames shot out of the tank and its damaged valve, hit the ground, and reflected around it, causing the tank to emit a roaring noise. Mark was physically fit and had no pertinent fire-rescue training or experience. He was knowledgeable about the properties of propane. He was a lifelong neighbor of Fink and knew the layout of his farm. The nearest fire station was a volunteer fire unit about seven miles away that was manned at the time.

RESCUE:

Mark went to the east side of the tractor and pounded on the cab door but did not see anyone inside. He called out Fink's name and heard a moan. He knelt and began to crawl west toward the sound, having to go underneath the burning vapors. He put his hood on and patted out burning stubble in his path.

He saw what he thought was a pile of burning cornstalks, but when he reached the pile, he realized it was Fink, who was lying . . . about 15 feet south of the burning tank. Flames rose about three feet off of Fink's body.

Mark attempted to pat out the flames with his hands. He then lay atop of Fink and seemingly smothered them. When he rose, however, the flames re-ignited.

Meanwhile, Duane arrived at Fink's farm. Smelling propane at the entrance to the farm, he turned off his truck's engine and coasted to a stop at a

point east of the tool shed. Fink's wife told him that
Mark was in the field with Fink. Duane approached
the field from the north end of the tool shed. The
vapors in the air had mostly burned off, but pockets
remained and would suddenly ignite. The tank and the
stubble in the field continued to burn. At the edge of
the field, Duane called out to Mark. . . . Duane ran to
Mark and joined him in trying to extinguish the
flames on Fink.

They were unsuccessful until they put dirt from
the field on him, but what remained of his clothes
continued to smolder. Duane used his utility knife to
cut away the fabric. Despite having difficulty
breathing, Mark and Duane rose and stamped out
burning stubble around Fink.

Mark then sat and held Fink's head in his lap.
Mark's son, who had arrived about the same time as
Duane, had retrieved a blanket with which they
covered Fink. Mark's son also retrieved a fire
extinguisher and used it to battle flames that had
broken out at some point on the tractor. Firefighters
arrived nine minutes after the 911 calls and
extinguished the remaining flames.

Fink was taken by ambulance and then helicopter
to a hospital, where he was stabilized. About an hour
later he was taken by helicopter to a burn center,
where he remained for 14 months, many of which
were in a drug-induced coma during which he
breathed with the aid of a ventilator.

At the time of the investigation, he had
undergone about 25 skin-replacement surgeries and

further procedures were probable. He had returned home and was able to walk but continued to undergo rehabilitation.

The report mentioned that the two candidates for heroism suffered smoke inhalation and minor burns. Duane was given oxygen in the field that day and taken by ambulance to the hospital.

Once the board reviewed the carefully documented case, it was not a difficult decision: bronze medals soon made their way from the Alcoa tower to rural Illinois. In May 2001 the arrival of the medals made news in the Freeport newspaper. Mark told the paper, "I'd do it again if I had to. I never thought of my safety and I know Duane didn't. . . . Before I entered on my hands and knees, I just knew Ted was in there and needed help, and by golly, I was going to do what I could to help him."

Duane told the reporter, "I would much rather have had something happen to me in the fire than to have just stood there and watched along the road. . . . I would not have wanted to live the rest of my life knowing I could have helped Ted" but did not.

In the end, the initial letter from Dr. Abernathy might have held enormous sway for the Carnegie Hero Fund Commission. In his conclusion, the emergency helicopter physician wrote, "There is little doubt that if it were not for the heroic actions of Duane and Mark Plock, Ted Fink would have been little more than a pile of ashes when the fire department arrived."

10

FIELD TRIP

✿ ACCORDING TO the coroner's report in early June 1948, the dead man had suffered a broken neck and crushing chest injuries. Death was probably instantaneous. The farmer had been driving his tractor on a sloping hill, moving dirt. The tractor suddenly overturned and pinned him under the seat. Family members recalled that one of his legs had been crippled in an earlier accident, so he was not able to jump clear. Another story in town was that the man had known a neighbor who was killed in a tractor rollover, and that he probably decided to hang on and not to jump, as the neighbor did, to improve his chances of survival.

Whatever the case, Elmer Fink was dead. His wife, Cora, had been in the yard at the time and saw the whole thing. That farming accident took Ted Fink's grandfather on June 3, 1948. It was shortly after 1 p.m., according to testimony given later that day by Coroner J. P. Schreiter. As Paul Turney, a trucker, was driving toward the Fink farm in Chadwick and topped a hill near the house, he saw the tractor go over. Running to the scene, he shut off the tractor engine and found

Elmer's leg caught under the seat. He and Cora called for help to free him from the machine.

Elmer's funeral was held at the First Lutheran Church in Chadwick on the Saturday afternoon after the accident. A quartet of women sang "Rock of Ages" and "Abide with Me." After the funeral, Cora took to the fields in her house-dress and underpinnings, for the growing season was well under way.

For decades the entanglement of men and machines has made farming treacherous. After mining, agriculture is the second most perilous profession, worse than construction. Between 1980 and 1995 nearly 94,000 Americans were killed on the job, and almost 12 percent of them were working in farming, forestry, and fishing. Yet agriculture, as defined by those three fields, employed less than one-half of 1 percent of Americans.

In 1995, according to a U.S. government study called the Traumatic Injury Surveillance of Farmers, there were about 196,000 farmer injuries that resulted in time lost working. Extremities were particularly vulnerable. Injuries most often involved a leg, knee, or hip, then the back or fingers, then the arm or shoulder. Most of the injuries occurred in the Midwest.

Farm operators and their families accounted for two-thirds of the injuries, with hired hands making up the rest. In other words, family farmers were injured at nearly twice the rate of the hired help. It may be that family members are more willing to take risks.

At the time of Ted Fink's accident, about three-fourths of farm fatalities involved tractors or other machines. The greatest single cause of death was just what had taken Elmer

Fink's life half a century earlier: tractor overturns. In the average year 110 American farm workers are crushed to death in tractor rollovers.

Every day about 500 farm workers are forced off the job by injuries of one kind or another. On average, 103 children were being killed annually while some 32,000 children and adolescents were hurt while working on farms, a 2002 National Institute for Occupational Safety and Health study showed.

The titles of the pamphlets published by this government safety agency are revealing: *Preventing Deaths of Farm Workers in Manure Pits. Preventing Entrapment and Suffocation Caused by the Unstable Surfaces of Stored Grain and Other Materials. Preventing Grain-Auger Electrocutions. Preventing Fatalities Due to Fires and Explosions in Oxygen-Limiting Silos.*

Preventing Scalping and Other Severe Injuries from Farm Machinery. A brief description follows the title: "This alert describes five cases of persons who were scalped when their hair became entangled around the inadequately guarded rotating drivelines or shafts of farm machinery driven by power take-offs (PTOs). Such entanglements of hair, clothing, or body parts kill and injure many farm workers each year."

Purdue University in West Lafayette, Indiana, established a program in 1979 to help disabled farmers and ranchers. It began after a paralyzed farmer called Purdue's Department of Agricultural and Biological Engineering asking for help in modifying his tractor so he could continue farming. That grew into a program in which the engineers in West Lafayette helped design an array of assistive devices for farm equipment. And that grassroots effort developed into the Breaking New Ground Resource Center, a world-renowned clearinghouse for rehabilitation technology for the farm industry.

At one point the center reached out to disabled farmers who had contacted it over the years, and put together a booklet with firsthand accounts by farmers who had overcome their disabilities to return to farming. The survivors volunteered to consult with other newly injured farmers; they were called Barn Builders.

One of the 102 disabled farmers profiled in the 2002 booklet was Douglas Anderson, who grew sunflowers and grain in North Dakota. He lost his left hand in a grain-auger accident, and afterward steered his tractor with a prosthetic hook. Larry Joe Yates, a fifty-nine-year-old cattle farmer in Indiana, became quadriplegic after a round hay bale rolled off a wagon and crushed him. After he lost a hand and part of his arm in a machine that picks corn, Charles Best, a seventy-three-year-old Barn Builder in Indiana, added steering knobs to his tractor and truck. He used rubber tips on his prosthesis so he could keep playing the organ.

Many children work on their families' farms, and in the 1990s more programs appeared for the "little sprouts" to learn how to handle themselves safely. *Progressive Farmer* magazine began holding farm-safety day camps in 1995, with 19 programs in 11 states. At one point the effort had grown to more than 250 camps annually in 38 states. One camp for youngsters was held in June 2005 at a farm in Gilman, Illinois, eighty miles south of Chicago. Gilman is in the heart of the old Illinois prairie, sitting at the intersection of the Illinois Central Railroad and the Toledo, Peoria & Western line. To help bring out crowds, a parade of 40 antique tractors was assembled, rolling along on a 20-mile route through Gilman and two nearby towns, Danforth and LaHogue. Radio station WGFA offered updates on the precise location of the tractors along the parade route at any given moment. One hundred fifty children were on hand, along with another 150 grownups.

The day was sponsored partly by the Iroquois Memorial Hospital in Watseka, Illinois, whose emergency room handles many rural injuries. "Although farming is a cherished way of life, it is full of potential dangers," said the hospital's brochure advertising the camp. "In addition to the most visible hazards—farm equipment and large animals—other dangers such as loud noises, pesticides, sun exposure and respiratory irritants can cause problems that may develop immediately or over time."

The children spent the scorching June morning running from booth to booth, trying out hands-on exhibits aimed at teaching them the dangers that lurked in their fields at home. A mother snapped pictures of her daughter at the horse-safety exhibit. A father took a photo of his son near a PTO, short for power takeoff, which is a handy and portable machine that uses an axle to power numerous farm devices. Fast-spinning and often exposed, the bare axle or the gears or the belts it turns are especially treacherous.

The U.S. Department of Agriculture made a 2002 farm-safety videotape, with open captioning for the deaf, which showed images of a man with a hook for a hand carrying bales of hay, and another man rolling his wheelchair around a pigpen, feeding the swine scoops of feed. A man named Alan Werk appeared on camera. "It was about 7 o'clock at night. We were picking and it was freezing. The cornstalks were freezing on the bottom and getting hard." He said the corn ears, frozen like popsicles, were jamming up the combine. "I got off to clean it out and I made the mistake of not shutting the PTO off. And I got entangled in the rollers—the front snapping rollers—and it cut both my hands off at the wrist and my legs got entangled in it, too, as I was trying to fight to get free. And I lost a leg above the knee."

Trying to drive the message home to the youngsters at the camp, one instructor showed how quickly a PTO can snag someone's clothing and yank a victim into peril. The instructor fired up a red tractor and flipped a switch, and the PTO began quickly turning two gears, spread six feet apart, with a rubber belt running between them. As they turned, the instructor moved a dumpy mannequin with shirt and pants into their vicinity. The pants caught and jerked the mannequin, which quickly became snagged in one of the gears. The demonstration worked a bit too well. When the next group of children showed up for the demonstration several minutes later, the instructor was still trying to free the mannequin from the gears.

At the Disability Awareness booth, twenty children sat in a semi-circle on haystacks, listening to an occupational therapist from Iroquois Memorial. She talked about how difficult basic chores can be when fingers or feet are disabled. To simulate hand disability, she had the children put on garden gloves and try, frustratingly, to open the twisted ends of a Smartie candy. Parents snapped photos. Later, with two or three fingers taped together, the children tried to pull Chex-Mix and little pretzels out of a medicine cup. More frustration, and laughter.

At another booth they learned about grain suffocation. It happens when a farmer becomes trapped in a tall silo or other storage vehicle and the grain funneling in begins filling up over his head. It is not an unusual accident. This form of being buried alive usually occurs when a farmer enters a bin as it is unloading, and gets sucked into the draining spout of grain. As the bin empties out the bottom, a person who falls anywhere into the bin can be pulled into that descending column of grain and trapped in a lethal avalanche, unable to breathe or fight his way out. It is like being inside the center of the sand at the top bubble of an hourglass, and then getting sucked in by the chute of sand formed as it sifts through the hole into the lower bubble.

Some farmers wear safety harnesses attached to ropes while they work around grain bins so that a co-worker can pull a suddenly fallen colleague to safety. Even that is not easy, and it gets harder by the second as more grain piles in atop the victim. At the farm-safety day in Gilman, the children circled a portable grain bin from Cargill, one of the largest agricultural companies in the world and a giant processor of grain. The bin looked like the top of a silo, a metal cone with a round opening the size of a manhole cover. A rope dangled from the hole. The exhibit was meant to simulate what a rescuer would encounter if he lifted the lid to a silo, saw nothing but grain up to the lid, and had to begin pulling on the rope attached to a farmer buried inside under heavy corn.

A sign on the mini-silo said, "In an entrapment, you are in a race you can't win. A flowing column of grain will pull you down to knee level in seconds and bury you within minutes." A graph showed a time-sequence of a man quickly sinking, as if in quicksand. At zero seconds he stood firmly atop the grainy pile. At fifteen seconds he was waist-deep. At thirty seconds his head was pulled just below the surface. At forty-five seconds his head was two feet below. At one minute he was fully six feet below the top and still being sucked down.

One by one the children put on orange safety gloves and tried their hand at pulling on the rope, which was attached to a 225-pound weight. The idea was to give them a feel for how hard it would be to extricate someone trapped and smothering in a grain accident. One boy pulled hard, veins showing in his forehead, his face flushed, and could not make the rope budge.

"Won't move," he said.

"I can't," said another, breathless.

Outside the bin was a poster, a representation of someone buried alive. A photo showed what looked like a yellow pile of gravel, and reaching out from the lethal corn was a single rigid hand, fingers bent as if clutching for something. The message read: "Think before you act. Don't add yourself to the victim list."

There was commotion at an exhibit with a massive green combine, a large machine used to harvest crops. It resembled a two-story house on fat-tread tractor wheels. The children assembled in front of it with anticipation. A stick-figure mannequin named Farmer Fred, with a black hat and blue overalls, was stuck in the ground just in front of the machine. He was placed right between two of the massive teeth sticking out from the head, or front end, of the combine. This machine is the workhorse of the harvest, rolling through ripe fields, trapping stalks between its jaws, knocking them down, and whisking the whole plant into the contraption, which, in a grinding whirl of corkscrewing metal, separates the golden ear from the leaves and stalk. It is quick, loud, and ruthless.

A man up in the glassed-in cab of the combine, fully fifteen feet in the air, looked down at Farmer Fred, a mop for a body and a crossbeam for arms with gloves on each end. Through a microphone blasted over loudspeakers, he barked to the children: "He is a dummy because he's standing in the combine's way. Watch what can happen if you don't pay attention."

The man started up the engine, which rumbled loudly, and turned on the blades, which had an ear-splitting whirr. As he pulled forward, the jaws of the combine grabbed the pants and legs of the stick figure, quickly gnawing them up. The outstretched arms, once parallel to the ground, convulsed up and down. A camp helper with a green baseball cap, sitting on a horse, looked on at the simulated calamity. The horse dropped its head.

"His legs are broke, and he's probably bleeding," yelled the man over the rumbling noise. This was a common and powerful demonstration at farm-safety days held throughout the country. Sometimes the mannequin was ground to splinters. Children often turned their heads away. Some cried.

Walking with a limp up to a microphone pole in front of the now-crippled Farmer Fred was a woman in her forties named Brenda Besse. She wore a short-sleeved, lime-colored shirt and blue jean shorts, which revealed that her right leg was artificial. Rising from her right white sneaker was a skeletal black tibia, made of metal, attached to a prosthetic stump that peeked out below the shorts. She stood in front of the children, purposely quiet for effect. They waited, staring at the false leg.

"This stickman and me had a very similar experience twenty, twenty-five years ago," she announced to the crowd.

The children sat cross-legged on the ground, some resting chins on their palms, their elbows resting on their knees. "I was working in a combine in a corn field, and instead of doing the correct thing—shutting it off—I got in front of it with it running." She explained that something had gotten clogged in the head of the combine, and she got out to investigate. Before she knew it, the combine grabbed her pants leg, then pulled her in. The children raised their faces from their palms and sat upright in attention, listening carefully. Their wide eyes repeatedly shifted from her mouth to her prosthetic leg.

"Them chains and them gathering fingers started chewing up my leg," she said. "Skin was flying, then bone was grinding, then it threw me—catapulted me forward ten to fifteen feet." The children stared. She explained that she pulled herself up, minus the bottom half of her right leg, and hopped back to the combine. "Back then, we didn't have cell phones," she said. She drove it out of the field to her truck, where she called her father on the CB radio and then collapsed unconscious.

"This thing is not a toy," she instructed the children, her voice suddenly cracking and her eyes welling up. She pointed to the stickman. "This could be your buddy or your brother or your friend—and they're dead. You don't come back from dead." She warned them to be careful all over the farm, particularly around the combines and other machinery.

After her short talk, the crowd dispersed, mumbling, and two boys lingered. They wanted to ask her questions. She told them not to be shy, to come over if they had something to ask. With a sticker on his chest that said "Quentin," one boy asked, "When you got your leg chopped, did it hurt really bad?" She replied, "Not at first," and he immediately walked away, satisfied. A boy named John asked how old she was when the accident happened. "Twenty-three," she responded.

Her family had had its share of farm tragedy, Besse recalled. Several years earlier, "my cousin backed over his dad with an auger wagon." The only way the young man found out that he had run over his father, she said, "He noticed a bump."

With direct raw talk, Brenda Besse purposely tried to scare the children safe. "These kids have no fear. You gotta instill fear in them." She kept an extra prosthetic leg in her truck and periodically gave it to the children during her talks. They would pass the leg around, child to child, as she lectured them, touching it and running their fingers along its hard, smooth plastic surface.

In the summer of 2005 Besse received an award from the governor of Illinois, a People Are Today's Heroes Award, which recognizes those who have made significant contributions to the state through their courage and perseverance in adverse circumstances. The award to Besse was presented by the Illinois director of agriculture in recognition of her work since 1991 in helping people injured in farm accidents return to their profession. She ran Brierwood Dairy Farm and raised champion Brown Swiss cattle in Hillsdale, Illinois. Some of her work was through a program called AgrAbility. More than seven hundred farmers in Illinois have been directly helped by AgrAbility caseworkers, and thousands more have received referrals to other services. Funded by the 1990 Farm Bill, the program has provided money for programs to help farmers deal with the emotional and physical consequences of their disabilities.

Aside from being an evangelist for farm safety, Besse has tried not to let her disability slow her down. Before her accident she attended college on a basketball scholarship. Many years after her accident, she got back into sports, playing in a special league of golfers in the National Amputee Golf Association.

Before the combine demonstration, one of the organizers of the safety day asked Besse if she would be all right watching the accident simulation just before her talk. "Well, I'd rather not see it. It really does bring it all back," she told the woman, but then she said to proceed with it anyway. After she spoke that day, Besse began thinking about her missionary work, fanning out around farm country and warning children about safety, and reflected: "I don't know why I do this. I get to a point in the talk, and break down."

As the children wandered around the grounds, a freckly red-haired ten-year-old boy named Dalton spoke to a girl next to him. "She's very lucky to be alive," he said. As she looked at the tall green combine, nine-year-old Halley responded, "I'm surprised it could suck somebody in. I've never gone in front of one before, but I definitely won't now."

Brenda Besse's disability did not define her, but her accident that October day more than twenty years ago has stayed with her. "I hate October," she said, combing her fingers through her short grey hair. "October sucks. I just want October away."

So many farmers suffered injuries to their legs that the National Easter Seal Society, a nonprofit disability group, prepared special safety tips for farming with paraplegia. The group recommended using a special "man lift" "to prevent excessive bruising, scraping or cuts to lower extremities when mounting or dismounting a tractor." It suggested keeping a cell phone or short-band radio whenever outdoors. And it advised using various wheelchair cushions while operating farm machinery to prevent skin breakdowns. It warned that dust, mold, and dander from livestock should be avoided because spinal-cord injuries could result in impaired use of the diaphragm or lungs.

It was about four years before her farm-safety camp talk that Brenda Besse and Mike Brokaw, an AgrAbility worker in Decatur, Illinois, heard through their contacts in the community about Ted Fink's accident. They called and visited a few times, checking on the Finks and asking what they might need. The Finks did not feel there was much AgrAbility could offer them that they could not do on their own. And they were uncomfortable with anything that felt remotely like charity.

Nonetheless Brenda took a liking to the Finks and tried to look in on them whenever she was in Carroll County. "Every time I'm up there, I go in to see Ted and Rhoda," she said one summer day, leaning on her metallic leg and standing against her truck. "Now *there's* a really brutal farm accident."

At a National AgrAbility training workshop in the fall of 2003 in Omaha, Nebraska, participants showed up to hear about the "Transformer," a wheelchair capable of raising and lowering its occupant from the ground to a standing position. There were also presentations on the "Ergonomic Evaluation of Commercially Available Operator Lifts for Farmers with Disabilities," "Orthotics and Prosthetics for Farmers and

Ranchers with Disabilities," and "Helping Hog Farmers Cope with Lung Disease." The same year the AgrAbility program in Madison held workshops for farm families on "Dealing with the Five Ds: Divorce, Death, Disability, Disaster and Disagreement."

When the staff at the AgrAbility program in Tennessee met with Lonnie Stockwell some years ago, they met a survivor from an attack by his 2,400-pound Blue Belgian bull. He could stand for an hour and ride around in his tractor, but he needed help designing and building a large hay-storage facility. AgrAbility helped build him one.

The AgrAbility group in Madison worked with Dennis Robinson, who was finishing his workday chopping haylage one day in 1998 when his sweater got caught in an automatic chopper box. In an instant he was pulled in headfirst and the blades began cutting into his arm, shoulder, and torso. He was rushed by helicopter to the Mayo Clinic, where during initial operations it seemed like doctors were operating on the Scarecrow from the *Wizard of Oz*. They kept pulling handfuls of hay from his stomach wounds. Robinson, whose dairy farm was near Prairie Farm, Wisconsin, lost most of the muscle in the left side of his stomach, and surgeons needed to take skin grafts from one of his legs to cover the missing skin.

Pairs of farmers, struck by the very same accident, may have very different outcomes. One day a farmer and his son were in a tractor that had an attached grain auger, a high metal chute that uses a corkscrew to funnel the grain from place to place. They contacted a power line as they drove underneath it, and in a split second one lived and one died. The son leaped clear of the tractor and survived. The father, though, was electrocuted because he tried to step out of the tractor. With the rest of his body in contact with the tractor, the moment he set one foot on the ground he completed a fatal circuit.

In Illinois two farmers were digging a deep irrigation ditch one day in the summer of 1986 when one of the big walls suddenly caved in on them. Brent Brightman, one of the men, was instantly buried in soil up to his neck. The second man was completely buried. A third man, who happened to be with them, called for help. When rescue workers arrived, they left Brightman buried while they frantically dug with hands and shovels to save the other man. After forty-five minutes they unearthed him and transported him to Community General Hospital in Sterling, Illinois. There he was pronounced dead by the county coroner.

"We didn't even bother with an autopsy," said Carollyn Fink, his widow. "He was either crushed to death or suffocated. They dug as fast as they could, but they could not get to him."

The following Sunday at 2 p.m. at the First Lutheran Church in Chadwick, a funeral was held for Vernon Fink, the elder son of Cora and Elmer Fink. At age fifty-five, Vernon had died in a farm accident, just as his father had. Sitting in the pews were Rhoda and Ted Fink, there for final farewells to Ted's only uncle. Ted's father, Arnold, was there, paying last respects to his brother. Arnold had previously lost a couple of fingers in a hog-house ventilation-fan accident.

"I always said I'd never marry a farmer," recalled Vernon's widow Carollyn. "Farming is a dangerous profession." She and Vernon lived on Cora Fink's old farm in Chadwick. It was right there in her front yard, near the road, that Elmer tipped over in the tractor.

I I

THE MATRIX

✿ WITH SIRENS singing to him about human regeneration, Yanni Yannas could not believe the turn of events for the
development of his artificial skin after the change of corporate owners in Kansas City. It was around 1981 that one of
his colleagues at MIT contacted Ewing Marion Kauffman,
the founder and chief executive officer of Marion Laboratories. Kauffman was intrigued with the artificial-skin experi-
ment under way at MIT and Massachusetts General Hospital. Marion Labs took on the license for Integra with high
hopes for this budding medical breakthrough.

Kauffman had been born on a farm in Garden City,
Missouri, in 1916, and his family later moved to Kansas City.
After serving in the navy during World War II, he came home
and took up work as a pharmaceutical salesman. In time he
was driven to start his own drug company; its headquarters in
1950 was the basement of his house. He named it Marion
Laboratories, purposely not using his last name for the corporate title so customers would not dismiss it as a one-man

company. First-year sales were $36,000. The company thrived over the years, moving out of the basement and making Kauffman a fortune, part of which he plowed into a passion for baseball. In 1968 he bought the Royals and returned major league baseball to Kansas City.

Yannas and the team at MIT felt they suffered a major league defeat after Kauffman sold Marion Labs to Merrell Dow in 1989. Before that, Ken Lynn, an attorney for Marion who had negotiated with MIT for the license to the artificial skin, said his company had developed an expensive "clean room"—similar to those in which workers wear gowns and protective caps in the production of silicon chips—to begin mass-producing Integra. Sometime around 1989 Marion submitted an application for the first Food and Drug Administration approval of an artificial skin. "There was a lot of excitement around Integra," including the production of promotional films about this promising new medical advance, Lynn recalled. But after the merger, Dow decided to focus on therapeutic pills. Integra fell under "wound care," a less-promising area for the new ownership.

Yannas vividly recalled the exhilaration he felt when he realized that what he had been formulating in his labs was not merely a new form of skin but a doorway to organ regeneration. He also remembered his concerns that his lack of a medical degree might cause physicians to dismiss his work. "You have to not pay attention to the lack of recognition from doctors," he said. His vantage point from outside the medical establishment allowed him to view a grand new vista he might not otherwise have seen. "You have to be an explorer and love it." Yannas said he was inspired by a Keats poem, composed by the English poet after he was deeply moved by Chapman's translation of Homer. In that poem, "On First Looking into Chapman's Homer," Keats compared his discovery of this new translation of Homer to the eye-opening experience of the European voyager who first confronted the Pacific Ocean: how it must have felt when the explorer spotted a vast body of sparkling, wavy blue that no one in his part of the world knew even existed.

Seeing his invention withering away, Yannas, who had spent his entire adult life in the laboratory, decided to try a new occupation: fund-raiser. He formed his own company, Morphogen, to try to find investors that would keep Integra on track by buying back the licensing rights. Yannas put up at least $25,000 of his own money. As he continued to seek a patron for his project, he renamed his company Extracell Corporation, whose address was the same as his house in Newton, Massachusetts. Yannas was president. MIT then struck a deal to share royalties with Marion Merrell Dow, which returned the licensing rights for Integra to the university. MIT then reassigned them to Yannas's companies in exchange for licensing fees.

It happened that an investor who specialized in high-tech projects heard that the license for the artificial skin had become available. Richard Caruso, who held a Ph.D. from the London School of Economics, had run a successful finance company called LFC Financial Corporation out of Radnor, Pennsylvania, since 1969. He was intrigued by Integra's matrix technology and the potential jackpot in regenerative medicine. The concept of applying a biomedical material to guide the development of the body resonated with one of Caruso's long-standing intellectual fascinations: mentoring. His doctoral research had to do with mentoring in the business environment, or how young workers develop after being taken under the wing of more seasoned professionals. Caruso's interest in mentoring had led to a book on the subject and to his forming the Uncommon Individual Foundation, a group dedicated to helping foster the development of mentors.

In 1989 Caruso, working with Yannas, established Integra LifeSciences Corporation as a vehicle for developing technologies that would allow the human body to regenerate tissue irreversibly lost because of disease, accident, or surgery. Integra, which served as a mentor, or guide, for skin regeneration, was the flagship product.

In the December 1992 contract that assigned the licensing rights for Integra to Integra LifeSciences, an escape clause made sure that Yannas would not again be left high and dry. The legalese read: "We agree that if Integra LifeSciences does not intend to commercialize any of the technology acquired from you, that it will at your direction and subject to the approval of MIT and the board of directors of Integra, license such technology to third parties who are not direct competitors of Integra LifeSciences. . . ."

Yannas, who became a senior adviser to the company and agreed not to compete with it, could finally breathe a sigh of relief. His more than twenty years' work appeared to be back on track.

Yet at this very time Dr. Burke, the burn surgeon who had helped Yannas develop the synthetic skin, was being questioned about the relative value of such a product. In an article for a surgical journal titled, "Who Is Responsible for Progress?" Burke made a broad argument for the value of medical advances by using his own experience in burn care as an example. "I believe the lessons demonstrated are global and pertinent to all medicine," he wrote. He acknowledged that "the repeated and invasive treatments needed to deal with an extensive burn injury have, with increasing frequency, been questioned because of the public's widening perception of a low probability for recovery." In the past, given that low probability, "extensive burn injuries were, and in some cases still are, treated with comfort measures only." In other words, efforts toward recovery were simply forgone in favor of merely keeping the patient comfortable until death.

Dr. Burke lashed out at such uninformed "inhibitors" of medical progress. "If no attempt is made to treat a disease, there will never be progress in the cure of that disease and future patients will be deprived of the benefits." He asked, Will a survivor be able to lead a happy, productive life and contribute to society? He reflected: "Survival is likely, but what is the quality of life? This is a most important question, for there is a widespread belief that burned patients may survive, but that they are destroyed as people, and their survival is not worthwhile." Concerned about these issues, Dr. Burke wrote, he had studied the long-term outcomes of massively burned patients treated at Mass General between 1974 and 1990. The group, he reported, showed an "unprecedented level of determination focused on getting well and returning to society." He added, "It is not that these patients did not have disability; the important fact is that their will and adaptive resilience overcame their handicaps."

More than 80 percent of the patients who recovered from massive burns ended up leading happy, productive lives and making contributions to society, Dr. Burke wrote. He related his own experience with a three-and-a-half-year-old girl whom he had treated at Shriners in Boston. She had been deeply burned over 86 percent of her body when her clothes caught fire. The accident happened before artificial skin was available, and she was treated in an experimental fashion, in which doctors lowered her body's immune response so that she could accept skin transplants from her mother. By the age of ten she was a "bright, outgoing child and today she lives a normal, healthy life." A twenty-eight-year-old electrician, burned over 80 percent of his body in an electrical explosion, later married, began working every day, and had two children.

"It is unthinkable to suggest that these people should not have been given the chance to survive their injuries," Dr. Burke declared. "However, the well-meaning and prevailing opinion is that patients with large, deep burns seldom, if ever, survive and if they do, have no quality of life. In addition, the cost of treatment is great, and because conventional wisdom states that survival is unlikely, it is logical to argue that it is unreasonable to squander scarce resources in a vain attempt."

Medical advances addressed what *could* be done, he wrote, but not always what *should* be done.

Five years later, in 1996, the Food and Drug Administration approved the use of Integra on burn victims and required that surgeons undergo training in the application of this unusual new product to patients. By the end of that year Integra was in the marketplace. Within a few years it had been used on more than thirteen thousand burn patients.

In Madison, Dr. Schurr had to go through the Integra training before he could use the product. He thought it had great potential to save patients he would otherwise have lost.

It also forced him to recalibrate his calculus in life-and-death decisions. "In terms of burn survival, Integra is absolutely life-saving," said the surgeon, whose burn unit was typically seeing victims with burns over 40 to 60 percent of their bodies. Integra greatly influenced Dr. Schurr's judgment that Ted Fink was treatable. "If we didn't have Integra, well, at some point in time it's your ethical and moral obligation to tell the family that this will be futile. If I had never heard of Integra, I'd have been of the futile mind-set with him," Dr. Schurr said.

His use of the word "futile" in this context had a specific meaning in the treacherous world of medical ethics. Bruce Zawacki, an emeritus associate professor of surgery and religion/social ethics at the University of Southern California in Los Angeles, took on this topic in a medical textbook called *Total Burn Care*, published in 2001. "The concept of futility and hopelessness in the care of a patient has changed drastically over the recent past. . . . Physicians have pushed . . . survivability to current levels where even in the youngest of age groups [who are often particularly vulnerable] extremely large burn victims can function and survive." In the context of medical progress, ethicists chew over the issue of just when treatment is useful or purposeful and when it is not. "We are finding that there is no simple definition of futility," Zawacki wrote.

But given the costliness of burn treatment, he offered a stark assessment: "The reality is that society is providing limited funds for the care of burned patients. It becomes a very difficult personal decision of whether the burn unit should focus on saving money and decline treatment of one burn victim to prepare for the next burn—or should resources be expended on a patient who perhaps has a poorer possibility of survival."

Zawacki succinctly described where burn victims fit on the scale of the afflicted, of all those in the world who suffer. His characterization will ring true to anyone who has spent time in a burn unit and taken in the foul odor of charred flesh, or seen the molten stretches of human hide, or the fingers or limbs reduced to bones, or the eyes gazing through featureless faces: "Burn patients are arguably the most severely injured and utterly vulnerable of human beings," he wrote.

Some patients may be moved to decide how far they wish to go with burn treatment according to their religious practices which teach that there are limits to this life and a need to seek a life beyond this one, Zawacki reasoned. And many patients will dismiss the extremes of treatment and continuing care to keep from burdening their family with large hospital bills. Some people may be influenced by the experience of close relatives who have had severe or terminal illnesses.

"The real question is what Ted would want to go through," said Dr. Schurr, recalling the decision-making process with Rhoda. "If Ted were sixty-five, wheelchair-bound, with dementia—that might be a different story. You have to ask yourself, would you want to go through this? You second-guess yourself—dream about these guys at two in the morning."

Dr. Schurr reflected on the amputations Ted faced. "I was distressed about the thumb. I thought we'd saved it." He recalled explaining that the procedure was needed, then producing a consent form for Rhoda to sign. "It's kind of awkward to have to say, 'Now, sign this,'" he said. Yet he found it easier to talk to Rhoda than to talk to Peter and Chris when they came to visit their father. "They were young," he said.

He believed that additional grafts several years after the accident would help Ted, but he noted that Ted "doesn't have the best donor sites"—meaning that the top layer of his skin was not as resilient and strong as the skin he was born with. Dr. Schurr also admitted that it was very painful to continue to harvest skin, which is done with a little humming machine that slices thin pieces from the surface of the skin. The spot where the skin is removed feels like "sliding into second base and getting this huge burning raspberry," he said.

Dr. Schurr had examined Ted's feet when he came to the clinic after his discharge from the burn unit. Essentially the severity of the burn had damaged his legs' ability to drain fluid. It began accumulating in his feet, which swelled enormously. They were spared by the flames (thanks to his brand-new size 14 steel-toed B. A. Mason work boots), only to be bedeviled by the limits of his body after recovery.

The boots came from a family-owned company, Mason Shoe Manufacturing Company, started by Bert A. Mason in the small logging town of Chippewa Falls, Wisconsin. He made a reputation for himself selling rugged leather boots for lumberjacks and river men that stood up to the elements. Over the years the B. A. Mason name spread up and down the Chippewa River and around timber camps throughout the area. The shoemaking company outlasted the depression and the leather rationing of World War II. During that war, people were so grateful to get any shoe that they would simply order a "man's" or "woman's" shoe and send along the foot size. The customers were happy no matter what style arrived.

The Finks tried compression socks designed to reduce swelling, with little result. "Compression socks are not a great solution, but we don't have a good solution," Dr. Schurr said. He offered one hopeful note: "I don't think his feet are in danger."

In Dr. Schurr's small office at the hospital in Madison was a framed, hand-stitched picture in blue thread from one of his patients. It read: "Life is not measured by the number of breaths we take, but by the moments that take our breath away."

The doctor sat there one day, five years after the accident, and reflected on Ted. "It was a frightfully hard case. I don't know if I'd be more inclined to do the same thing or less. You get a sense that maybe I was young and foolish back then. It's a heroic save, but he's a very disabled man. He's limited—but he is back with his family."

On his door, along with handwritten notes and birthday cards from his daughters, the surgeon had a copy of Robert Frost's "The Road Not Taken." He said he likes to ponder the crossroads everyone faces in life. Its final stanza:

I shall be telling this with a sigh
Somewhere ages and ages hence:
Two roads diverged in a wood, and I—
I took the one less traveled by,
And that has made all the difference.

12

LIGHT AND SHADOW

It rained during the night
And two puddles formed in the dark
And began chatting.
One said,

"It is so nice to at last be upon this earth
And to meet you as well,
But what will happen when
That brilliant Sun comes
And turns us back into spirit again?"

—Hafiz

✿ AMONG THE stunning images of the terrorist attack on the World Trade Center, few were more gripping than those of the poor souls leaping from the sky to their deaths to avoid the searing heat and gathering flames. Fear of fire is primeval. "There is only one thing in the world I am afraid of," said the

Scarecrow in the *Wizard of Oz*, resonating that ingrained terror, "a lighted match." The Roman Catholic church recognized Joan of Arc as a saint after she was cruelly burned alive. The dramatic murder of the nineteen-year-old French heroine in 1431 continues to inspire films, novels, poems, and plays.

Ted Fink beat the flames people everywhere dread, and survived with an eyewitness account. "When the propane was escaping the tank, I could see the vapor, a white cloud going under the tractor. I threw the cab door open and jumped out. I jumped into the biggest wall of heat. It was an inferno. I tried to roll on the ground. I had my good greasy overalls on, and since I rolled on the ground and the cornstalks were burning, I burned everywhere. I laid there, undoubtedly unconscious, until Mark came and grabbed me. Once we got out of the flames, I was conscious again. I recall him hollering something. I was aware of things. You can't imagine horrible until you're lying there in a field, flesh on fire, burning like cinders and smelling your own burning skin. It hurt so much, it's not conceivable, the pain."

After the accident, Rhoda could recite the short list of places her husband had not been burned. "Feet, back of neck, groin, a spot the size of a dinner plate across his chest," she said one day. Hearing that, Ted added: "There wasn't much left of me."

The last thing he could recall was getting into the helicopter, the feel of the stretcher, the whirr of the blades, and the sounds of the frantic rescuers. He was loaded onto the chopper in a brown field at an intersection outside Lanark. The area was once called Lost Grove, near a snaking body of water still called Lost Creek. Ted then faded to black for months.

"When I did come to, I thought only a couple hours had elapsed. Waking up out of a coma, you don't know where you are. I didn't realize a half a year had passed. Most people say I'm a one-and-only because I'm not supposed to be here."

When he finally awoke, what helped Ted endure the remaining months in the hospital was the promise of returning, in some fashion, to his life's passion, farming. From the time he was a boy there was no doubt how he would spend his life. It's what the Fink men did. His father, Arnold, farmed. As did his father, Elmer, and his, William, and his, John. All farmed within a twenty-mile area their whole lives.

Now that legacy was in doubt, and Ted was already working against the tide. In less than two generations the number of farms in America had shrunk by two-thirds. From a peak of nearly seven million farms in 1935, the number had fallen to just above two million by the early 1970s. The rate of decline has slowed since then, but farms, and farm life, have clearly been disappearing. The small family farm, though usually unprofitable, has held on as a real driver in the national agriculture market. Even as larger corporate farms have changed the landscape, small operations still accounted for about a third of total agricultural production in the late 1990s.

His whole life Ted had been practical, taking care of what needed to be done day to day. He did not often pause for reflection. Since the accident, though, prolonged pauses had been forced upon him. One spring day, several years after the accident, he reflected on what the Fink family tree had been doing, deep down, all those years. "All we do is plant a seed and turn sunlight into a different form of energy," he said. "We take sunlight, a couple ingredients, toss in water—and look at what we made!" He said fertilizer and soil and seed all combined elements that lured warm vitality from the baking sun, that great indispensable ball of fire. Plants cannot grow in darkness; they wither in shadow. Farmers harness that vital sunlight to grow grain and corn and fruits and vegetables. In time that produce serves as energy to sustain people. Ted was using nature's oven to fill dinner plates. Ted Fink fed people the sun.

Pondering their livelihood, Rhoda thought about the earth's perfume. "In the fall or spring, when you do deep tillage, it has an odor that's all its own—you'll drive down the road and say, 'God, that smells good.' I always wanted to be close to Mother Nature. With every season you yearn for this satisfaction that I made something out of nothing with Mother Nature."

"You don't farm to make money," Ted added. "It's just a way of life. This country is fortunate that it's so vast that you can do this. It makes you feel like you're doing something worthwhile. I go to bed at night and I have a lot of blessings."

They are blessings of creation that St. Augustine, a theologian whose confessional life account was one of the earliest autobiographies in Western literature, recognized in this way: "What greater or more wonderful spectacle is there, or where can human reason better enter into a dialogue with the nature of things, than when seeds have been planted, shoots laid out, shrubs transplanted, grafts inserted. It is as though one were questioning each root and seed, asking it what it can do and what it cannot do; whence it derives the power to do it, or why it cannot do it; what help it receives from its interior power and what from exterior help and diligence. And in this dialogue we come to understand how neither he who plants nor he who waters is anything, but God who giveth the increase. For that work which is applied exteriorly is fruitful only by the action of Him who created and ruled and ordered all from within."

A little over a year after returning from the hospital, Ted was running into a serious problem: he needed more land. Certain fixed costs of farming can be spread over greater and greater acreage to realize more profit. He and Rhoda owned about two hundred acres, the land Cora had purchased long ago in Lanark. Like many small farmers, Ted and Rhoda rented most of their land, another eighteen hundred acres or so. Land had gotten so expensive that renting was the only option.

Ted admired his father, following him through the fields and tagging along at the Carroll County Fair, proud that his father was a fair official in the all-important tractor-pull event. But he regretted that his father was too conservative by not borrowing to buy real estate when farmland in the area was dirt cheap. "Father would never buy ground," Ted recalled. "He saw too many people go bust because they were overextended. In hindsight, he should have bought some more." The couple of hundred acres Ted and Rhoda owned were inherited from his father after he died. His older brother, Gerald, got a similar amount of land adjacent to Ted and Rhoda's. But, like many family farmers who couldn't afford to buy more land given the vulnerability of farming to weather and market cycles, Ted had to rent land from others to grow enough crops to scratch out a living.

Since the accident, Ted had not gotten out around town much, and many people who knew he was hurt in the explosion did not know he was back farming. It was then that the entrepreneurial side of Ted, the man who drove to see the founders of Wal-Mart and Wendy's, resurfaced. To alert neighbors, stretched miles and miles apart, that he was back, Ted began radio advertising in the fall of 2003, paying one hundred dollars a spot to WCCI, 100.3 FM, in Savanna. The station served a six-county area in northwest Illinois and eastern Iowa. It played country music, carried broadcasts of high school football games, and brought the latest in farm news. "The best in new hit country," ads promised. "25,000 watts serving you in Illinois and Iowa."

Beaming over both sides of the mighty Mississippi came Ted's appeal for land—"If you've got tillable cropland you'd like to lease out or sell, call Ted Fink in Lanark"—and then gave his home phone number. "He's looking for good cropland in Lanark and the surrounding communities. If you can help him out, give him a call."

Another: "Ted Fink of Lanark is asking for your help. He's interested in buying or leasing good, tillable cropland in Lanark or the surrounding area. If you'd like to put those idle acres to work for you, give Ted a call."

And: "Friendly Ted Fink of Lanark is on the lookout for good, tillable cropland to buy or lease. If you've been wanting to scale back on your operation, give Ted a call . . . and work out a deal. He's looking for land in Lanark and the surrounding area. Talk to Ted."

The radio appeals were not generating leads, though. It seemed as if Ted had broken some kind of farmers' protocol by advertising. "Depending on who you talk to, the community frowned on it," he said. "Farmers usually don't advertise—sometimes you'll see little ads in the paper, but not much else."

He decided to try another scheme. He ordered dozens of fat red pens printed with his phone number and the slogan: *Ted Fink, Chris Fink—Stewards of the Land.*

The pens included their phone numbers and a plea for land to rent. That summer, concerned his longtime banker did not fully appreciate that he was healthy enough to run the operation and that he intended to pick up where he had left off, Ted had Rhoda help him from his walker into the driver's seat of the blue minivan. It was a laborious process as he dragged his feet slowly. Rhoda stood by to steady him and to catch him—if she could—if he began to fall. It made her nervous letting him drive, and sometimes she even tried to keep the keys from him, particularly when she thought his pain medicine might make him unsteady.

Once inside the van, Ted drove to Chadwick and parked outside the office of Metrobank, a big agricultural lender with eighteen branches in Illinois and Iowa. The place, which used to be called Farmer's State Bank, offered loans for livestock feed, machinery and cattle, and property.

Using his walker, Ted made his way to the desk of the senior vice president of agricultural lending and stood there in his hunched posture. Bart Ottens, who wore a thin tie and had straight bangs that covered his forehead, looked up, stunned. Ted reached down to the pen box on Ottens's desk and poured all the pens out on the desk. He then deposited a fistful of the red "Ted Fink" pens in the box. "I'm back, Bart," he said.

"I never expected he'd be in here again, physically and mentally capable, after what he'd been through," Ottens recalled. "He said he was mentally capable of running the operation and going to pick up where we left off. He said he was back in the captain's chair and that Chris was capable of operating the place." After hearing the authority and certainty in Ted's voice, Ottens felt reassured that the Fink place remained a good risk. "It made us feel pretty good about it, that he was back. You can rest a little easier," the banker recalled thinking. Metrobank continued making loans to the Fink farm.

Chris, in his early twenties a bull of a man like his father, had taken over most of the work of running the farm. Throughout the summer, working in a white shirt and blue jeans, his arms and neck would bronze in the blazing sun. When his wife called him for lunch and he went inside and removed his green John Deere cap, his forehead was alabaster, protected by the bill of the cap. Ted's skin remained white all year as he sat inside ordering seed and equipment, contracting with buyers, and handling the books. Ted's face was lit by the glow of his computer at night as he monitored such matters as the development of a soybean industry in Brazil. That helped him estimate where prices were likely headed and allowed him to time the sales of his own crops accordingly. "We never used to worry about what the corn crop in Argentina was doing," said Rhoda. "It's a family farm, but now a worldwide market."

Chris suddenly had two big responsibilities at once. In September that year Samantha Fink joined the family, Ted and Rhoda's first grandchild. She had big blue eyes and thin strands of strawberry-blonde hair on a mostly bald head, like her grandfather's. Meanwhile Chris had fully taken on what his dad used to do: he prepared and fertilized the soil, planted the crops, repaired all the equipment, and, when the season was ending, he harvested. The Finks began hiring a part-time helper for busy periods—at one point Deanna's older brother, Aaron. Now in his early thirties, Aaron had worked for a trucking company and didn't have the seasoning of farmers in the area. Ted always worried about taking on inexperienced workers who might quickly grind through costly equipment. "People with no experience will tear up more machinery than it's worth," he said.

And being without a combine at a critical time could be disaster. From the time the crops were ready, the Finks had to harvest every soybean and ear of corn within about four weeks' time. The farm had silo space for only about half the harvest, so the rest of the corn and beans had to be trucked away for sale. The corn grown at the farm was used mostly for livestock feed and for export to Europe and Japan. Soybeans ended up as oil in numerous foods. The Finks would all work long hours at harvest time, sometimes using headlights after nightfall. They could not always quit before then. If the weather is favorable on any given day, farmers like to keep going. The next day it might rain.

In the seasons after the accident, Ted also had to resort to retired farm hands, men in their sixties and seventies. After about four weeks the old men would be exhausted, and Ted would start scouting for replacements. One year it was a retired farmer from the nearby town of Milledgeville. He was over seventy and had had heart trouble and surgery. "We have had a ragtag mix of people," Ted said. That spring Ted welded a ladder that Chris attached to one of the combines so that Ted, with help, could climb up into it. Gripping one rung at a time, he got to the top, swiveled around, and sat with a thud

and a sigh behind the wheel. He began running the combine
a bit during harvest to help out, operating a joystick inside
the cab with the two remaining fingers on his right hand.

Being in the combine and rolling through the fields as
its blades chopped through the stalks and leafy bean plants
was pacifying for Ted. He could contemplate his future plans
for the farm: whether to grow genetically modified crops,
what mix of corn versus beans he should employ, whether
there would be certain insects that needed to be extermi-
nated in the coming year. "Basically you're a season ahead—
'scheming,' as mother calls it," he said one day, referring to
Rhoda.

Ted had been planting corn in thirty-inch rows, but
while out riding the combine one day he decided the next
year to try rows spaced only twenty inches apart. He hoped
thereby to increase the yield of each acre. "Doesn't seem like
much," he said, "but it will more than pay for itself." The way
he figured it, with each cornstalk closer together, the leaves
would "canopy," overlapping and shading the ground underneath. Weeds wither in shadows. "I have many hats I have to
wear," Ted was fond of saying. "One minute I'm a seed expert, then a nutritionist to keep the soil in good shape, then
a worldwide economist. Since the 1970s, what happens in the
rest of the world affects us here."

That particular season, the third since he had left the
hospital, he decided to plant half his acreage in corn and half
in soybeans. The year earlier it had been two-thirds corn and
one-third beans. The change made sense from a labor point
of view. "Less bodies needed to grow soybeans," Ted reasoned. On their farm, corn produced 160 bushels an acre,
soybeans only 50. Planting more beans would mean fewer

crops to process and haul and store, and fewer rickety retirees to count on.

Even if Ted could get inside the combine on his own, he decided not to. "I don't go anywhere without somebody being nearby," he said. And he began carrying a cell phone with him everywhere. He admitted, "I don't do a tenth of what I used to. Basically, all I have to offer is experience because, shit, I can't do it physically. What's very bad is sometimes I think I can do things, and I find I can't."

Although he had recovered some strength and dexterity, he still could not manage much more than a slow shuffle with the use of a walker. His legs got stuck, bent at the knees, as a result of a condition called heterotopic ossification. Basically an inflamed joint, like the knee, begins to fuse over with bone. When Ted's knees locked, he lost the maneuverability to get out of his chair. His scars continued to shrink. The pins-and-needles sensations persisted. He had open wounds on his legs, rear, and torso that stubbornly refused to heal. Rhoda kept wrapping him every day in the green and yellow bandages. He grew frustrated with sores that would not close and simply oozed. "Every day my clothes weep," he said.

Because of the bone-fusing problem, he could barely bend his elbows, meaning he lost most of the ability to rotate his hands. "I can't turn my palms up," he said one day. Then he contemplated what that loss meant. Looking at his granddaughter, he said, "I can't hold the baby."

His feet, the one body part fully spared the flames, were no better. Ted's feet essentially accounted for the unblemished 7 percent of his body. Because of the severity of the burns to his legs and his ensuing inability to drain fluid properly, the extreme swelling in his feet persisted. His shoes no longer fit.

One day he and Rhoda drove to a cobbler in Sterling, a large town to the south, who wanted $450 for custom-made shoes. They ended up going to Rockford, the second-largest city in Illinois and an hour-and-a-half drive away, where an orthopedic and prosthetics store agreed to take his regular shoes and stretch them. When that did not work, they picked out a pair of oversized blue slippers called Apex Ambulators, which were fastened with Velcro-like straps. Ted's new shoes.

The Finks' mailbox was just across Maple Grove Road, not twenty feet from the driveway of the house. But it was still too far for Ted to walk safely; he could not avoid an oncoming car. To get the mail he needed to get in the minivan and drive to the other side of the road. There he could reach into the mailbox—painted John Deere green, with a yellow deer on each side. Coming back to the house in the cold months, he would pass a wooden snowman in a barrel, with a sign on it that said, "Winter is a bushel of fun."

When he returned one day in that winter of 2003, in the front hall he walked by a thin wooden table with Rhoda's farm Snowbabies, little figurines on tractors and a red barn. In his office, in the front of the house, where he could spot the mailman making his delivery, Ted had a half-dozen model tractors on shelves. He also had aerial photos of the farm going back for years. A local airplane photography firm had flown over the farms for decades, taking shots for farmers who wanted them. Every Fink farm had them posted proudly on the walls. They showed how the landscape had evolved. Picture to picture, pigpens turned into fields. Silos rose and disappeared. Houses gained additions. In one shot on Ted's wall there was just the old farmhouse; the new house, the butter-colored one the Finks were then living in, was not in the picture.

In addition to the computer and a calendar, Ted kept just one artifact—his trophy from the 1965 tractor pull. It was heavy, all metal, with a man sitting on a tractor at the top, where normally there is a shiny sprinter or figure skater. The years have left their tarnish on the tractor and its driver. If asked, Ted would acknowledge that questions were raised, that people thought it fishy that the son of the superintendent of tractor pulls also became a frequent champion. "But that doesn't explain the tractor pulls I won in other places," he would say. "Tractor pulling was our life," Judy recalled.

On the wall in Ted's office was a framed poem, given to him by Chris.

I believe a man's greatest possession is his dignity and that no calling bestows this more abundantly than farming.

I believe hard work and honest sweat are the building blocks of a person's character.

I believe that farming, despite its disappointments and hardships, is the most honest and honorable way a man can spend his days on this earth.

I believe farming nurtures the close family ties that make life rich in ways that money can't buy.

I believe my children are learning values that will last a lifetime and can be learned in no other way.

I believe farming provides education for life and that no other occupation teaches so much about birth, growth and maturing in such a variety of ways.

I believe many of the best things in life are indeed free: the splendor of a sunrise, the rapture of wide open spaces, the exhilarating sight of your land greening each spring.

I believe true happiness comes from watching your crops ripen in the field, your children grow tall in the sun, your whole family feel the pride that springs from their shared experience.

I believe that by my toil I am giving more to the world than I am taking from it, an honor that does not come to all men.

I believe my life will be measured ultimately by what I have done for my fellow man, and by this standard I fear no judgment.

I believe when a man grows old and sums up his days, he should be able to stand tall and feel pride in the life he's lived.

I believe in farming because it makes all this possible.

—Author unknown

A summer or two after the accident, Ted had undergone a release procedure on his neck to stop a skin tightening that had been tugging Ted's lower lip downward. Integra, the lifesaving prosthetic blanket of skin, gave him a second shot at life, but the outer layer of his skin, which comes into contact with the world, had begun to turn on him. Because his neck skin continued to contract, his lips could not fully close, so he had to keep a bottle of Coke or Sprite with him at all times, sipping periodically to keep his mouth from becoming unbearably parched.

One day in the fall of 2004, when Chris felt Ted was not using the combine correctly, he grew so exasperated with his father that he shouted over the loud engine, "I'll be glad when Samantha is old enough to run this thing." That was shortly after Ted crashed his tractor into a parked tractor Chris was in, knocking Chris's toolbox into the machinery and mangling it. Chris barked at him for his inattention. Then Ted turned to his son with a response neither fully expected.

Ted told his son, "Sometimes I get engrossed in something because it helps me forget for a while how I am."

13

BOUNTY LAND

These are the gardens of the Desert, these
The unshorn fields, boundless and beautiful,
For which the speech of England has not name—
The Prairies.

—*William Cullen Bryant, 1833*

🐾 THE OLD FINK FARMHOUSE was built on a parcel of
160 acres of Illinois property that the federal government had
deeded to a soldier in the mid-nineteenth century. At the
time, officials in Washington were seeking to encourage settlement of the prairie by handing out free deeds to soldiers
who placed their lives on the line in sundry military skir-
mishes. It was an early army-recruitment tool: Uncle Sam
needs you, and has some land for you to back it up.

The deed for the property in northern Illinois showed
that the 160 acres were granted on July 1, 1854. And rather
than the recipient's being a Civil War veteran, as some in the

Fink family thought, he was actually a mercenary in the War of 1812.

This is how the nation's breadbasket came to be filled. Between 1847 and 1855, Congress in four separate acts parceled out more than sixty million acres of public land to more than half a million veterans and their widows and other heirs. Some historians believe that an additional purpose of these acts was to fill the frontier with legions of burly, seasoned soldiers who could help in ongoing efforts to rid the land of Native Americans, who happened to be there first. This was the Wild West, the frontier, the land that deeply frightened the civilized gentry among the colonial descendants in the East.

The threat of Indians, along with the deep-seated suspicion that the treeless prairie was inhospitable to both plants and people, conspired to keep settlers away. Accustomed to dwelling among the forests of Europe and eastern North America, European newcomers needed wood to make their log cabin homes and to heat them. "Timber was considered such an important commodity that counties were not allowed to form as governmental units until residents could demonstrate that they had access to sufficient timber to support development," observes Kenneth Robertson at the Illinois Natural History Survey in Champaign.

The barren landscape, filled with wispy stemmed plants but lacking anything as substantial as a tree trunk, was striking to poets and writers alike. Washington Irving, the author of "Rip van Winkle," once wrote, "To one unaccustomed to it, there is something inexpressibly lonely in the solitude of the prairie. The loneliness of a forest seems nothing to it. There the view is shut in by trees, and the imagination is left free to picture some livelier scene beyond. But here we have an immense extent of landscape without a sign of human existence. We have the consciousness of being far, far beyond the bounds of human habitation; we feel as if moving in the midst of a desert world."

Early settlers were horrified by the incivility of the environment. There were swarms of buzzing, biting insects. With no hope of shade from the scorching sun, summers were miserable and dry, winters bleak. As far back as 1673, the Canadian explorer Louis Joliet remarked: "At first, when we were told of these treeless lands, I imagined that it was a country ravaged by fire, where the soil was so poor that it could produce nothing. . . . There are prairies three, six, ten, and twenty leagues in length and three in width, surrounded by forests of the same extent; beyond these, the prairies begin again, so that there is as much of one sort of land as of the other. Sometimes we saw grass very short, and, at other times, five or six feet high."

The wind caused waves on the surface of the vast ocean of grass, and one type of wagon the pioneers used even borrowed a nautical term, the "prairie schooner." Without trees or other natural landmarks it was easy to get lost, and even on horseback a rider could not always find the horizon amid the high grass.

When the vast fields of swaying grasses turned brown and brittle, pioneers lived in mortal fear—way out there in the endless countryside that could quickly become one vast tinderbox.

The prairie fire was a constant dread for early settlers in Illinois. Started by lightning or Native Americans, prairie fires were so common that every one to five years, some environ-

mental scholars believe, any given parcel of land was probably burned. Periodic droughts, high temperatures, and strong
winds provided an ideal environment to ignite and maintain
fires. The flat topography of the Midwest helped them spread
easily.

Uncontrolled fire mercilessly scorched crops, fences,
buildings, livestock, and even the settlers themselves. "Due to
the high danger of fire, pioneers slept with one eye open
from the time of the first killing frosts in the fall until snow
covered the ground," according to the history of one Illinois
county. "The season, called the Indian Summer, which com-
mences in October by a dark blue hazy atmosphere, is caused
by millions of acres, for thousands of miles around, being in
a wide-spreading, flaming, blazing, smoking fire, rising up
through wood and prairie, hill and dale, to the tops of low
shrubs and high trees," as one Illinois pioneer recorded in his
journal in 1817. People were so fearful that the flames would
spring up rapidly and consume all in their path that some
came to call the prairie fire the "Messenger of Death."

Another Illinois pioneer, Nehemiah Matson, a self-
styled scholar of the nineteenth century, recalled one blaze
from November 1836: "A fire started on the Spoon River
about 10 o'clock in the morning, and with a strong southwest wind, it traveled about ten miles per hour, passing between West Bureau and Green River, having a front eight
miles in width, and its roaring could be heard for many miles
distant. Before sundown, this fire had burned to the banks of
the Rock River, where Rockford now stands, passing over a
country of about sixty miles in extent."

Caralee Aschenbrenner, the Lanark historian, described
the "red battalions of flames" that could be seen in the distance

as they swept widely across the prairies, adding that they would rage for days until a rain put them out or dampened the grass sufficiently that it would not burn. For their protection, she wrote, the settlers found it necessary to make "fire breaks" by plowing furrows about a quarter of a mile apart, to create a buffer zone that had no kindling. Yet in a furious wind, burning tumbleweeds sometimes were catapulted across the firebreaks. The balls of flame confounded the settlers' fire-suppression techniques.

Beyond fire, another natural deterrent to human interloping on the terrain was the ground itself. The tough soil, which had been tilled by glaciers sometimes to phenomenal depths, was so rich that the early settlers called it "black gumbo." Yet it remained a trial to plow. Kenneth Robertson once described the soil belowground as "a dense tangle of roots, rhizomes, bulbs, corms and rootstocks. . . . The roots of the big bluestem [grass] may be seven feet or more deep and switchgrass roots more than eleven feet deep. Some of the roots die and decompose each year, and this process has added large quantities of organic matter to the soil. This is one reason prairie soils are so fertile."

Farmers long tried to plow the prairie under in order to plant crops, but the ground proved so hard that they would sometimes have to bring in a soil specialist, the "sodbuster," who charged two to three dollars an acre in the early 1800s. Even so the work was slow and grueling, and wore out teams of oxen.

Settlers from the East found that the cast-iron plows they had brought with them did not work in Midwest soil. Their plows had been designed to handle New England's light, sandy earth. The rich Midwestern soil clung to the bottoms of plows, and every few steps a farmer had to stop, scrape off the soil, and begin again. The pioneers were discouraged from farming.

But a young blacksmith from Vermont named John Deere looked into the problem and in 1837 designed a plow using steel from a broken saw blade. It was highly polished and helped clean itself as it turned the slice of a furrow. He tested the new plow on a farm near Grand Detour, Illinois, just miles from Oregon, where Cora and Elmer Fink would later elope. Grand Detour lies at the bend of the Rock River, at a spot, according to Indian lore, that the river found so beautiful it had to turn around to look at it again. (Along one twelve-mile stretch of the Rock River are the Illinois towns of Oregon, Grand Detour, and Dixon, the boyhood home of President Ronald Reagan.) A decade after he developed his first "self-polisher" plow, John Deere was producing a thousand plows annually.

With the elimination of Indian warriors, settlers felt safer in Illinois and began arriving in great numbers. The John Deere company would eventually become a giant producer of tractors and other farm implements.

In Illinois alone there had been 21 million acres of prairie before European settlers arrived. Roughly 2,300 acres of prairie remain in the state. This phenomenal disappearance of prairie, to a tiny fraction of its original acreage, occurred also in Indiana, Iowa, Minnesota, Wisconsin, and Missouri. As railroads developed after the Civil War, Illinois farmers gained a means of transporting their produce, and that encouraged the conversion of more and more land to farming. "Railroads changed the dynamic of subsistence farming to agriculture for money," said Kenneth Robertson.

By 1900 most of the Prairie State was no longer prairie. Lost forever in the process was a vast grassy ecosystem, along with most of its animals and plants. A noted nineteenth-century bird researcher, Robert Ridgway, was an eyewitness to the environmental upheaval. He made his first visit to an area called Fox Prairie in June 1871. On a visit just twelve years later, he left this account: "The changes which had taken place—instead of an absolutely open prairie some six miles broad by 10 miles in extreme length, covered with its original characteristic vegetation, there remained only 160 acres not under fence. With this insignificant exception, the entire area was covered by thriving farms, with their neat cottages, capacious barns, fields of corn and wheat, and even extensive orchards of peach and apple trees. The transformation was complete; and it was only by certain ineffectual landmarks that we were able to identify the locality of our former visits.

"We searched in vain for the characteristic prairie birds. Upon the unenclosed tract of 160 acres, dickcissels, Henslow's buntings, yellow-winged sparrows, and the meadowlarks were abundant as ever; and running in the road, now wallowing in the dust, then alighting upon a fence state, were prairie larks; but equally numerous were also the detestable and detested European house sparrow, already ineradicably established. . . . We left our beautiful prairie with sad heart, disgusted with the change, however beneficent to humanity, which civilization had wrought."

Before the ravages of man, this land—which eventually brought forth a native son named Ted Fink—was itself victimized by fire. About 8,300 years ago the weather pattern grew much hotter and drier, part of a larger climatic shift that prompted the retreat of glaciers. Much of the forest in the Midwest simply died, except along the banks of streams. Prairies spread. When rainfall increased, the forest was able to reestablish itself. But during droughts, prairie plants took over previously forested regions. Trees and bushes have fragile living tissue above ground, which is harmed in a roaring fire, but most prairie plant life has deep roots that hibernate in the fall and winter.

This tug-of-war eventually favored the prairies, which are one of the youngest ecosystems in North America. Most ecologists believe that prairie vegetation in the Midwest would have largely disappeared during the last five thousand years had it not been for persistent and periodic burning. One of the necessary ingredients to make a successful prairie, it turned out, was fire.

Modern grasslands developed only about six thousand years ago and now comprise approximately 16 to 40 percent of the world's land area. Grasslands are important for agriculture, as most of the food produced worldwide comes from these areas.

Yet the prairie has persisted and thrived because of recurring fires blazing hot above ground, raging at up to 1,250 degrees. Soil proved a good insulator. "Prior to European settlement, the vegetation of much of the Midwest was a shifting mosaic of prairie, forest, savanna and wetlands that was largely controlled by the frequency of fire," Kenneth Robertson's research shows. Fire was regulated only by the occurrence of natural firebreaks: rivers, streams, and wetlands.

Illinois, outside of Chicago, has remained largely rural. The state spans about four hundred miles from its tiptop (farther north than Boston) to its bottom (farther south than

Louisville). Illinois is part of a vast grassland in the middle of North America that once stretched from Indiana to Nebraska, to Texas in the south and Canada in the north. The prairies of northwestern Illinois, where the Fink clan settled, were called the Driftless Section.

Researchers have been surprised by the resilience of prairie vegetation. Plant specialists involved in prairie restoration have reported that they can revive a "prairie matrix," a soil that will grow some of the most forgiving of plant species. Their presence and subsequent thriving pave the way for fussier, more fragile species that flower on the prairie. Over and over it has been shown that it takes two to three years to establish the prairie matrix. Man's attempts to reseed other things with a matrix have left decidedly mixed results.

Several years after Ted's accident, Rhoda purchased a book titled *A Practical Guide to Prairie Reconstruction*. Her sister-in-law was a soil scientist, and the two had been talking for years about ways to resurrect the prairie, particularly the bygone flowers of the old plateau. The book had a whole chapter on how important it is, when trying to establish a remnant of prairie, periodically to set the garden afire.

Rhoda worked long hours planting, watering, and weeding her flower beds around the house. She had yet to try to plant the lost flora of the prairie, but what she did plant offered petals of calming hues along the foundation of the butter-colored house. She wheelbarrowed her tools from clutch to clutch and worried over her flowers in the dry summer months.

"I always wanted a prairie here," she said.

14

THE SEASON OF '04

ᵂ EACH TIME something went awry, the Trak 350 computer box, tucked in the corner of the cabin above Chris's shoulder in the John Deere tractor, let out an ear-splitting beep. Then another, and another. If the wheels suddenly stopped turning properly, if a stone became lodged, if one of the seed bins had emptied out—*Beeeep! Beeeep! Beeeep!* The alarm would not be ignored. Each time Chris had to stop the tractor, shut off the alarm, locate the problem and fix it, put the tractor back in gear, and begin rolling through the field again until the computer box objected. He was sitting in a glassed-in cabin, the size of an old photo kiosk, a story above the ground. As he made his way through the stubbly field, he pulled a planting machine behind. It was a rack of twenty-four yellow plastic bins, spaced evenly twenty inches apart. As he pulled the rack along, it poked holes in the ground to precise depths and instantly deposited a single kernel of seed corn. This kind of precision assured that cornstalks would grow in exact position, like rows of soldiers.

On the windshield was brown dust, kicked up from the dry fields. Up close the tractor and planter were massive, but from a distance the rolling machinery looked like a dot on the lonely plain, with a faint halo of dust around it. Inside, country music played in the cab. After a time Chris came to a stop and grabbed one of the fifty-pound sacks of Pioneer seed corn from a pallet. He poured out of the corner of the bag, refilling each of the bins. Then he climbed back up into the cabin and started rolling again. It was a solitary day, with hours behind and hours ahead, all alone in the cabin, acres from anyone. It was early in the planting season, April 2004. Days and days just like this stretched ahead.

From the side of the field, in his blue Dodge Caravan, Ted sat quietly, with oversized sunglasses that fit over his regular glasses. Against the black bugeye lenses Ted's face seemed whiter than normal, ghostly in the shade inside the van. Although it was a hazy April day, with a light grey sky, Ted's eyes remained sensitive to light. He had had to do more "windshield surveillance" since he could not get around and move inside the fields very easily. When Chris returned to the pallet of seed sacks, Ted yelled to him from the van, "We're going to have to set the planter deeper."

"Deeper?" hollered Chris.

"Deeper. The planter is riding on top of too much garbage," Ted answered. His worry was that the planter was not close enough to the surface of the soil, that it was riding unnaturally high on a floor of stalks and plant residue. If the seed was not planted deep enough, it would not grow properly and might die. He worried about acres of spindly, withered stalks.

Chris doubted the old man. Wearing his green John Deere cap, blue jeans, and sleeveless T-shirt exposing tan, beefy arms, Chris got out a pocket knife and carefully unearthed a first seed, then a second, checking how deep they were. Ted was right; they were not down far enough. Chris set the planter deeper. It was a mistake that Ted with his years of experience would not have made. But he didn't criticize Chris. "There's certain things you just can't see from the tractor seat," the father consoled.

The beeper kept sounding partly because of Ted's decision to plant the cornrows closer. "With narrower rows, I keep running over stuff," Chris said. Just then a large stone got stuck between the prongs of the machine, and the beeping began again. The Trak 350 showed that Chris had planted 59.6 acres at that point, going about five miles per hour. He was anxious to get some ground behind him that day. Ten days earlier he had begun planting, and the first day he was rained out. The next day, rained out again. Even with the Trak 350 and the fancy new planting machine, which cost more than $100,000, he could plant only about 20 acres an hour, and he had fallen behind. About 10 percent of the corn seed had been planted at that point, and timing was crucial. You cannot plant too early. Northern Illinois may have brutal cold blasts well into the spring, but corn can stand frost more easily than soybeans, which is why it was being planted first.

The vagaries of weather place planning and farming routinely at odds, and sages of the soil will tell you that it's better to learn not to resist nature. After it began raining the previous Sunday afternoon, Chris called it quits and went inside, frustrated that the day's work was foiled yet again. He sat

down at his desk and got to work on bills and other paperwork. Then he looked up from the desk and over at Samantha. After weeks of fits and starts, she was at it again, up on all
fours, trying to crawl. Knowing she was obsessed with eyeglasses at the time, Chris removed his glasses and put them on
the floor a few feet in front of her as a temptation. His daughter then crawled over to them. Because he had been rained
out, he got to see that milestone in his daughter's young life,
her first crawl. "Worked out nice," he said.

As planting continued, Ted and Rhoda began talking about
scheduling release surgery to restore some movement to Ted's
elbows. But they had to wait because the wounds on his rear
end just would not close up. "I've got open wounds on my
butt," Ted explained. "Tushy," Rhoda said, correcting him.

The planting needed to proceed, the weather was not
cooperating, and Ted was not limber enough to help Chris.
He tried to concentrate on ways he could be helpful. "If I'm
sitting in the tractor—well, they don't go too fast, so I'll be
okay," he said, consoling himself that the postponed surgery
would not prevent him from running a tractor at least.

He spoke despair. "I used to be a driver. I worked. And
I expected the same of everybody else. I never expected people to do more than I did. But now that's gone. I ain't got that
kind of energy anymore. Chris has taken all of that on now."

Gingerly, Rhoda asked: "Don't you think, Ted, you took
your strength and physical stamina for granted?"

"Well, yeah," he replied. "You don't know what you
have until you lose it. Some people in my shoes would never
leave the house."

Rhoda said, "Luckily you had something to do. If you had had a factory job, what would there be left for you to do?"

Sitting in his office in the front of the yellow house on Maple Grove on a grey day that May, Ted spoke about his general condition. "Ma wanted me to have surgery because it helps. . . . I told her I've got other things to do." Like many burn patients, he was reluctant to continue enduring skin grafts. It was painful in places where surgeons carve even the thinnest spots of skin. "They pulled a spot from my hip, and it took four or five times before it would take on my back. They take a meat slicer to 'harvest' a piece of skin," Ted recalled. And Oxycontin, a pain-reliever he took, did not help, he said. "I've got so many sores still open—I won't live to see them heal."

While he was in the hospital, Ted had so few healthy spots to donate skin to himself that doctors had to resort to an innovation called cultured skin. A patient's own top layer of skin is removed, then injected with animal cells—in Ted's case sanitized mouse cells—to stimulate rapid growth. A few small samples from a patient can quickly grow into several square feet of new epidermis. Doctors then apply the cultured skin. The process has had mixed success.

After he left the hospital, over time Ted gained fifty pounds. His appetite returned, and he was much less active than before the accident. Coming home nearly skeletal, he said, "They wanted me to put on weight." But within two years he found that the cultured skin did not stretch very well. "So now that I've gained weight, the skin tightens and . . . as cultured skin tightens, it tears, erodes away, and you get these big sores. So I eat just a little bit. I'm having to eat less to keep the skin from stretching." His T-shirt that day had blood all over the back; his wounds were bleeding. Ted had no feeling on his "flank," so he had no way to sense when the blood was oozing and staining his T-shirt.

His eyes had tears. "Some days everything hurts; some days only one thing hurts." On the computer desk in his office was a little plastic urine bottle with a handle and "Fink" written in black ink. He had to keep it on hand for times when no one was in the house to help him in the bathroom.

On a Tuesday, Ted and Chris drove to an equipment auction in Oregon. The sale, which began at 9 a.m., was held by Northwest Equipment. Rows and rows of equipment were parked outdoors. Ted had Chris haul their John Deere Gator, a green all-terrain vehicle with four tires with fat tread. Ted rode it up and down the aisles of equipment, taking in the smorgasbord of machinery. There were tractors and loader tractors, harvesting combines, hay balers, mulchers, skid loaders, backhoes, corn heads, grain heads, choppers, spreaders, bottom plows, chisel plows, rotary hoes, seeders, and crustbuster drills. A featured item was a handsome 1989 John Deere 8760 bareback tractor with 4,830 hours on it.

Ted and Chris were hunting for a reliable old combine. Ted brought a box of the "Ted Fink" pens and placed them at the cashier's desk for people to take—hoping still to drum up business. In less than an hour they were all gone. When Ted and Chris left, the only things they were hauling home were their Gator and an old plow.

Rhoda placed an inflatable pillow under Ted's bottom as he bent to take a seat in his John Deere 610C, the one he was in four years earlier when the flames engulfed him. The pillow was to help protect his legs and bottom from further degradation. Chris had placed big wooden blocks on the metal steps to help Ted step up into the cabin before Rhoda climbed up with the pillow. It was a three-person mounting job, but Ted was in.

Atop his orthopedic throne, Ted began moving piles of dirt. He had dug them up earlier to make room for a massive grain scale. He pulled on a lever inside the cabin with his right hand. He had two bandages on his left hand and one across the knuckle of his right hand, its two remaining fingers helping grip the levers in the tractor. That crippled hand was the one Grandma Cora, many years before, had tried to train him to favor.

The week before, Ted and Chris had torn down one of the silvery, conical silos to make room for the new scale. They wanted to build the scale that summer to weigh the grain they would harvest in the coming months. Until that point the grain buyers, the large companies that loaded the harvests of area farmers onto barges and floated them to the next middleman, had scales, but the Fink farm did not. Over the years Ted could estimate the weight of his produce pretty closely by the content of his truck. But he did not know it to the precise pound, and the grain merchants did. Ted had a nagging feeling that, for his protection, he needed to know for sure. Chris had begun taking some contract work for other farmers. Come harvest, the scale would allow them to sort out precisely how much was hauled from the Fink farm and how much from the others.

On a farm about five miles away, Ted found forty-foot I-beams that had been used on an old bridge. The plan was to bind them together to make eighty-foot rails, then run a wooden track between the rails. The truck would drive onto the track to be weighed.

Anticipating the welding work that was to come in a few weeks, Rhoda knew that Ted had ears tuned for fire. He could tell how well the welding was going strictly by the sound, by the hiss or squeal as the bright blue flame struck metal. It irritated Chris when Ted instructed him to make changes in the way he was welding because he didn't like the sound.

The scale would also help Ted determine which fertilizer, crop, and soil mixture was most productive. A scale of this caliber would run $120,000 if bought new. But Ted Fink always tried to do as much as he could solo, without help from anyone. "Store-bought" to him signaled laziness. "We'll build ours for just under $15,000," he said.

Through his contacts, he found a man who sold scale electronics, the brains of the device, on the side. The man offered the electric kit Ted needed at a big discount, $4,500 new. A brown UPS truck brought several boxes over several days. The brains arrived in stages, and Ted and Chris bolted and screwed the contraption together. Ted called the man, a few counties away, to notify him that the kit had arrived. Two weeks later he paid the bill. There was no prepaying, no deposit, no credit card numbers exchanged, no contract. The nod-and-handshake form of commerce—trust—was still alive in Illinois.

As they worked on the scale, Ted began to fret about his soybean crops. The leaves were yellowing and cuffed, both alarming signs of distress. His green acres were becoming yellow acres. He called a couple of seed distributor reps to come out the next day and look at the fields in the morning. He thought maybe insecticide from a nearby field had landed on his crops and was damaging them. And he had a backup plan. If he thought the rep was simply giving him a line to cover himself, Ted was prepared to call a "university guy from down south," an academic troubleshooter, to come look at the beans.

On a Sunday night, the Fourth of July, Rhoda and Ted sat on their back deck and watched fireworks splitting the night sky over the fields surrounding their home. Ted worried about what was happening to the soybeans beneath the night sky. Even in the dark, the soybean plants were visible in the moonlight and the fireworks, waving, like swells and tides, all around the house.

"I broke down and got one," Ted said. "I lowered myself to using it." Using his walker had become an increasing struggle. He could manage it, but he moved like a snail. Walking unaided was impossible. It was too dangerous, and slow, trying to walk while leaning on Chris or Rhoda or Peter's arm. He talked over the situation with Bob, one of his landlords, who was eighty-six and had had one for forty years himself, after he was stricken with polio. "Bob, I'm fighting it," Ted said. "I don't want to feel like I need it. A wheelchair." Bob looked at him and replied directly. "Don't fight it—accept it."

After shopping around, Ted decided on the Invacare Patriot model that ran more than a thousand dollars. Rhoda thought he should get the black model; Ted wanted lavender. The wheelchair had a lightweight aluminum frame and weighed only twenty-nine pounds. It also had a built-in amputee attachment that, the wheelchair maker's marketing materials said, "provides quick and easy amputee setting." It offered a variety of wheel and tire choices.

Ted might have spent more time fussing over it, but he had a bigger problem with another vehicle. He realized belatedly that his grand plan to narrow the cornrows, the one aimed at producing more corn per acre, faced a major problem. The axle on the pickup truck, which the Finks used to spray the crops, was not wide enough for the tires to clear the closer rows of corn. Driving the spraying truck through as it was configured would crush the young corn plants under the tires. Hours at a time, Ted mulled the problem over. Within days he came up with a solution. He bought new wheel rims for the pickup that moved each tire about six inches out and gave him an extra foot of clearance.

Samantha, who was now crawling admirably, watched her grandfather lean on his walker at home as he moved from the kitchen table to his office. She observed keenly. Then the toddler crawled over to his walker, reached up for its poles, gripped hard, and pulled herself unsteadily erect. Once upright, she leaned on the walker and used its sturdy structure and its rolling wheels to scoot along slowly. Unable to steer the thing, she propelled herself along on a straight path until a chair or wall brought a frustrating end to the excursion.

Within weeks she began walking upright without grandpa's walker, and one day waddled over to the kitchen table where Ted was sitting in his new wheelchair. She raised her arms, her big blue eyes imploring. He looked down and saw her.

"Now, honey," he said, "you know grandpa can't pick you up." She kept her arms raised to him. And he repeated, "Grandpa can't pick you up." Because his arm joints were so stiff, he could not clasp his granddaughter in his hands. Walking in from another room, Deanna saw what was going on and lifted the child onto her grandfather's lap. He cooed at her.

On another day the newest member of the Fink family worked her way over to a box in Ted's office that said Oxygen Concentrator. At night the rumbling machine fed oxygen into a hose, twenty or so feet long, that Ted ran into the living room. It attached to a mask that helped him breathe at night. He slept in the La-Z-Boy with the mask and the tube. Samantha was teething that summer. In bare feet, shorts, and a tank top one day, Samantha got hold of the oxygen tubing, raised it to her lips, and began gnawing.

After lunch another day, Ted suddenly set down his fork, which had an extra-wide handle to make it easier to hold, and tried to bend down to look under the table. He thought he had dropped a pain pill and was worried Samantha might find it. Because he was not agile enough to get down on the floor, he asked Rhoda to look.

Ted's legs by then were constantly bent at the knees because of his inflamed joints fusing over with bone. He could not lie flat in bed any longer, so at night he began sleeping in the recliner in the living room. Ted's La-Z-Boy was sitting on a platform made of fiberboard, about four inches high. The extra height made it easier for him to flop into and rise out of.

More surgery might have helped with some of Ted's problems, but he was not much interested. "To do it right, I should probably have about fifteen more surgeries," he said. "Not going to happen. I don't think the old bod can take that many more surgeries. Each time I think I come out a little worse than when I went in." Rhoda thought more improvement was possible, though, and wanted Ted to reconsider future surgery.

"You could probably dress yourself," she told him one day.

"I still couldn't put my pants on," Ted answered. "Surgery could help, but they beat the hell out of you in surgery."

Rhoda dropped the subject. Later she said she had seen how painful the skin-graft operations and recovery were. "I don't want to nag him," she said. "I'm not the one who has to go through it."

In Ted and Rhoda's bedroom was a framed Olan Mills photo of the family, taken in the fall of 1999 just before the fire. Peter had come home from college for the portrait. Rhoda had bought the boys new shirts for the photo. Peter's was green, Chris's light brown. Ted wore a crisp white shirt. All three wore ties. Rhoda was in a red floral dress. She wore hoop earrings and a necklace with pearls. Framed by the sons and sitting next to her sat Ted, with thick grey hair, broad shoulders, and a thin smile under his bushy, salt-and-pepper mustache.

Rhoda picked up the photo from the dresser one July day and inspected it. Two things struck her. She was still annoyed at Chris for not getting rid of the toothpick he was gnawing on before the photo was taken. And then she looked at Ted, studying her husband's old face. "His mustache," she said. "I miss the 'stache."

One day that summer the Finks decided to have lunch at the old farmhouse. Deanna was in the kitchen preparing it as Ted sat at their kitchen table, waiting. He removed his light green golf cap, which he used to protect his balding head from the sun. On his scalp were two bandages, one round, one rectangular.

Ted didn't see them, but there were bloodstains inside the golf cap. Nine-month-old Samantha, sitting in Ted's lap, reached for the hat. Ted handed it to her. She was at that age when everything went in the mouth. Chris suddenly spied the bloodstains on the inside of the cap, and without Ted's noticing, he reached over and took the hat from Samantha. He handed it to Deanna, who set it on a table out of the child's reach.

Fall came. "I've got to do something about my feet— they're so swollen," Ted said one day. His feet were enormous, stretching even the Apex Ambulators. Rhoda and Ted began almost daily visits to Swedish American Hospital in Rockford for two and a half hours of lymphedema treatments for chronically swollen feet. Nurses bandaged wounds and then wrapped each toe individually, aiming to compress and squeeze the tissue to help it drain excess fluid. While there Ted also attended an outpatient wound clinic that specialized in helping people with chronic sores that refused to heal. There they began taking photos on the progress of the healing every five to six weeks. Appointments ran three hours. They removed dead tissue from the sores and made new photographs.

After a time, Ted began bringing red, blue, and green "Ted Fink" pens to the wound clinic, asking the nurses which one they liked, in what he called "market research." He said,

"They all take it very seriously." As for his feet, they recommended Ted elevate them to help with the swelling. He refused. "I want to live the way I used to," he said. "Medicine is a fine thing, but it does nothing more than buy you time."

With effort, practice, and proficiency, Rhoda had been able to reduce Ted's showers from three hours to an hour and fifteen minutes. He could maneuver more, and he could hold the little spraying showerhead for her. The bathroom in the new house was roomier, too. Rhoda luxuriated in the extra space, calling the place the "party shower." By then the couple could split shower duties, much as they had coordinated to drive the old Nova together.

Rhoda could not believe how long it had been that some of Ted's wounds had failed to heal. "If they had told me at the get-go that five years later he would have open wounds, I would have called them liars," she said one day, exasperated. "Ted's bandages are pretty stinky by the end of the day."

The months wore on. Harvest was nearly complete on a Saturday that October. It was bitter cold, forty degrees and windy. High up in a combine harvester, Ted was chopping down stalks in front of him and golden kernels were piling up in the vast bin behind him. They pressed against the back windshield just behind Ted; the wall of corn rose and rose, inching higher and higher and eventually covering the entire window. It was loud and dusty. It was getting late in the day, and there were acres and acres left to do.

Ted suddenly looked directly ahead and saw a grey bunny. It was hopping up ahead, right in the path of his loud, whirring machine. He slowed the harvester to let the rabbit run out of the way. But rather than hopping to safety, it hopped only a few feet forward, dead ahead of the whirring blades. Ted slowed again, and the rabbit hopped another few feet ahead. After this happened three times, the rabbit finally veered and ran to another section of the field, out of harm's way.

The mysterious cuffed soybean leaves had a simple resolution. They were the result of a mix-up with one of the spray tanks filled with weed-killer. After the tank had been used with one herbicide intended to kill weeds competing for the soil with the corn plants, it was rinsed out and filled with herbicide designed to protect the beans. But herbicide meant for corn can kill soybean plants, among other unwanted species in a cornfield. After consulting with the seed company man, Ted figured out that they had not properly cleaned all the herbicide from the tank when changing from field to field. Thus an issue of sanitation imperiled the family's livelihood in 2004. Rains helped dilute the poison from the beans, but the Finks learned a hard lesson. "We gotta be sure the tank is cleaner next time," Ted said.

Later that week Ted tried to pick up the microphone from the radio in the combine when Chris called him, and dropped it when he tried to depress the little button to speak. The small receiver, the size of a cigarette pack, fell and then bungeed up and down on the coiled cord. "I went to get a cell phone the other day," Ted said. "They're all so small. That's fine if you've got cute little petite fingers—that work. I need a wide one I can hold."

Stacked on the kitchen table one day that December, the first day of winter, were Ted's magazines: *Prairie Farmer, Agrinews, Pro Farmer, Top Producer,* and *Farm Journal.* In another stack were Rhoda's magazines: *Radiologic Technology, Better Homes & Gardens,* and *Southern Living.* Between caring for Ted and keeping house, Rhoda had no plans to return to work. Among the few remnants of her old life were a monthly lunch with her former hospital colleagues and her subscription to the bimonthly radiology magazine. Work, for her, was out of the question just then.

It helped a bit that Ted received disability assistance through Social Security and an Illinois state insurance program. By the time all the paperwork was done, Ted's medical bills had exceeded four million dollars. Most of that was paid for through an Illinois state catastrophic health insurance plan, after his private insurance was wiped out.

Tapping away on his computer in the office one day, surrounded by the aerial photos of the farm, often taken when the place was bountiful, in full flowering vegetation, Ted was doing research, looking for new hope for his skin. He found a 2001 article from a journal called *Skin Wound Care,* titled "Using Skin Replacement Products to Treat Burns and Wounds." A doctor in the Madison area was working on something improbably titled "immortal skin."

Ted said he was unsure what he was looking for, but he felt it was important to investigate anyway. "I want to keep up with things. My skin may crap out."

On his desk, in the corner, was the 1965 tractor-pull trophy. He was fleeing to the Internet under the growing weight of limitations. "All those jobs I dreaded doing, I wish

I could do now," Ted said. He missed menial chores, the unappreciated joys of being a grunt. What he wouldn't give, he lamented, to be shoveling out the grain bin again when the blazing sun made it one hundred degrees outside, and hotter inside, and his job was to dislodge the corn melted into the silo walls with an ax.

He lowered his head, looking into his lap, which was resting in the wheelchair. "I wish I could walk."

With Rhoda's help, Ted opened the door of his minivan, then turned slowly to swivel around into the seat. Once he was rested on the seat, Rhoda walked around to the passenger side. They had this choreography down pat. Ted reached for the assistive device attached to the ignition key and pulled on the switch. The motor started, and he backed the van out of the garage. He grabbed the adaptive knob on the steering wheel and turned out of the driveway.

In the distance was what looked like a small mountain. He drove toward it and within a few minutes arrived at his neighbor's farm, at the edge of the enormous hill. It consisted entirely of chopped corn. Chris and another man were maneuvering four-wheel-drive tractors in a crisscrossing pattern over the top of the heap, compressing and squeezing the air out of the corn, which was intended as cattle feed. They crossed and crossed, driving by each other, motors rumbling. The idea was to keep moisture out so the corn would not spoil.

Ted watched for quite a while, fixed on the corn heap. Then he pulled the van up near the edge of the hill and sat there for a few moments. And then the 1965 tractor-pull champion reawakened.

Suddenly Ted punched the accelerator pedal. Dust kicked up from the rear tires, and the blue minivan lunged forward, headed directly at the hill. When the front tires reached the base, they began to climb up, lifting the van up the side. But within seconds, barely a quarter of the way up, the tires just spun, unable to get traction.

Ted put the van in reverse and backed off the hill. Still backing until he was a hundred feet from the edge of the hill, he braked, threw the van into drive, and punched the accelerator again. The van hit the hill straight on and began a second slow ascent. It got a little farther than the first time, but then stalled as the tires spun helplessly in the corn residue. Ted eased off the hill. He decided not to try again.

Looking down from the top of the hill and watching his father trying to beat a path to the top in a van with handicapped plates, Chris shook his head. There was his obstinate father, trying to run up the giant mound in a vehicle meant to haul suburban children. But Ted recalled how it was when he and Chris used to drive the tractors compressing the mound. "I used to do this," he said, and he drove slowly away.

15

THE SONG OF THE FINCH

🐦 THE BLACK PONTIAC STREAMLINER sat under the lean-to, under a coat of dust. The hood ornament had the menacing face of a Native American warrior with a swept-back feather headdress. The signature of the post–World War II model Pontiacs, the chrome chief kept watch season after season as the leafy crops, stretched to the horizon, rose and fell around the Fink farm.

Ted had hoped to show off his prize at car shows and take it out for an occasional joyride. But after the accident he could not get in it, much less drive it. The Pontiac had no power steering, power brakes, power anything. "The boys drive it every now and again," Rhoda said one day, "and we try to keep the mice out of it."

Ted had spent most of his life in cars and fields. His lecture to Rhoda all those years ago about the mating dance of corn was part of Fink family lore—usually to the annoyance of the grown Fink boys. Like most young adults, they didn't much care about their parents' early, cuddlier days. When he came into the room and overheard his parents reminiscing about it one day, Chris rolled his eyes and protested, "Not the corn-sex story again!"

One day Rhoda placed a bird feeder in the front yard, just outside Ted's office window in the front of the house. She had seen a beautiful cardinal flying around, and she wanted to attract him for close viewing. Instead the little red feeder drew mostly finches, the namesake bird of the Fink family. The purple finch, feasting on the feeder one day, has a lively, warbled song. Some of the telltale songs of the finch family, birdwatchers have noted, seem to be little hymns to grain and crops. A common call of the house finch is a long drawn-out *wheattttt*. Scientists have also recorded finches singing lyrics that sound like references to the European breakfast cereal: *"Mostly Muesli, Mostly Muesli, Mostly Muesli."* That lyrical finding may be found in a book called *The Beak of the Finch*. It describes how an individual finch uses its unique songs to locate and identify its species for mating and other communal purposes. One observation: "The average male has a very limited repertoire. He has just one advertisement for himself, which he sings over and over all his life. . . . In fact, most males sing the song of their father. . . . Singing the right song is important: a finch that learns the wrong song is in trouble."

Ted Fink's song, throughout his life, had been farming, and his sons learned to whistle in kind. Chris said he does not resent his college plans being upended by his father's accident. It remains a dream deferred, and one he cannot soon pursue again anyway, with a young daughter and a wife now dependent on him. No matter. "Somebody's gotta stay home and run the place, or we wouldn't have a place to run," Chris said, resonating with perfect pitch his father's matter-of-fact tone.

After the fire Peter interrupted college in Ohio and farmed for a year. Then he moved to suburban Chicago to complete his college degree in computing. After graduation he took a job in the computer-services department at the college, but he soon tired of the work, the traffic, and big-city life. Wrong song. Peter returned to his father's farm in Lanark to help Chris run the place.

The disruption to his sons' lives clearly bothered Ted. "Dad's always trying to apologize," said Peter. He tried to appease his father, telling him that the changes were good and opened new doors for him. As for his father's heroic struggle back from the fire, Peter said, "I don't know if I could do it myself."

In a way, Ted, like Icarus, took a fall when he got too close to the sun. The farmer's encounter with the fireball came as a result of the potent brew of a chemist who crammed explosive energy into a can. Ted's second chance at life came from the handiwork of another chemist who wove molecules into a blanket of synthetic skin. In between the lab work and the machines and tools of men fell Ted Fink's life.

Rhoda's lonely months in the burn unit led her to believe there were spiritual reasons why her husband survived. "I saw people who were not as burned as Ted and not as old, and they would die," she said. "I don't know if you'd call it—" she paused, hunting for the word. "I don't know if you'd call it . . . theological, but his being here just seems meant to be.

"Ted's glad to be here, even though he's got problems." As she pondered some of the losses they had suffered, she recalled some of the gains. Ted no longer needed a breathing tube. He could feed himself. Since he had become more agile and able to wield the showerhead, his bathing routine was down to about an hour.

"If at any time in the first two to three weeks I'd have said, 'I don't think the end result is going to be good for Ted,' they'd have, as they say, pulled the plug," Rhoda said. "And I don't think anyone would have blinked.

"The kids and I had a lot of discussions about it. Ted and I have had lots of talks about it. If his kidneys had failed or we had a big problem, that would have been a different story."

Ted tried to show Rhoda his appreciation, going with Peter one day to J. C. Penney and buying her a gold and diamond ring the first Christmas after he returned home from the hospital. The vows had grown much heavier since he had tucked the first ring in the glove compartment a quarter-century earlier.

After the accident, Rhoda one day put her feelings about marriage to paper. "Ah, marriage," she began. "We got married so young we didn't know that there could be problems in a relationship. Marriage is: a lifetime commitment before God and family; having someone to always be there for you whose commitment, faith and trust never wavers; having a best friend; having someone to share and trust your most intimate thoughts and desires with; growing together so that each of you can be the best person possible.

"The line 'in sickness and in health' is a tough one to get your head around. There was never a moment that I thought about bailing out after Ted's accident. We have shared so much

over the last 30-plus years—love, kids, death of loved ones—
and have created such a bond that there was no question that
with God's help, we would stick it out and make the best out
of a really crappy situation. Marriage can be hard work!"

Rhoda had learned to be the stronger one, and she had
her Teddy back.

Time, in northern Illinois, is often measured in crop heights.
According to a popular saying, the corn is "knee-high by the
Fourth of July." During the summer of 2006 Ted endured
several stubborn infections, and his health began to slide. One
Sunday night late that August, when the corn was eye-high
and with Rhoda at his side, Ted put his head down on his La-
Z-Boy, closed his eyes, and never awoke.

The tolling of bells opened his funeral at the First Evan-
gelical Lutheran Church in Chadwick. The Reverend Marcia
Strahl made a few kind remarks about Ted, about how he had
a passion for watching things grow, whether crops or trees or
his children. She said that when she would occasionally visit
the farm, Ted was at the ready for her, with lists of questions
about scriptures. He was particularly interested in the book of
Genesis, she said, the biblical chapter of origin that chronicled
the flowering and peopling of the world. Reverend Strahl said
she was unsurprised that Ted took such an interest in that
book. "Land is part of our life," she told the filled church.

Ted was laid to rest in Chadwick Cemetery on an over-
cast Wednesday around noon, in a plot at the very edge of the
property where a tall row of ripened corn from the adjacent
farm stood watch over the burial. Rhoda chose one passage
to read at the funeral service. It was from St. Paul's letter to

the Romans, and read in part: "We stand and rejoice in hope of the glory of God. And not only that, but we also glory in tribulations, knowing that tribulation produces perseverance; and perseverance, character; and character, hope."

Ted's death certificate listed complications from burns.

A year and a half before he died, and some five years after his accident, Ted one day considered the wisdom of Rhoda's decision to save him. He paused for a time, and then became animated. "You can't condemn someone for making choices," he said. "You make them and you don't know if they're good or bad. It's done and you hope for the best. I can't begin to put myself in her shoes."

Thinking of himself, he added: "It's like a person with breast cancer. It may be all cleared up one day through treatment. And then five years later it can come back to kill you. You thought you had it won. But then it comes back to get you. Was treatment the right way to go? You'll never know.

"When you reach the point that you can't do what you love to do, you have to admit defeat. You need to have a purpose and have to be useful. If you can't live on your own and are always 100 percent dependent on other people, then you turn into a burden.

"With modern medicine we keep people alive whether they want to be or not. That's a call that needs to be made by the one that's gonna live it, and usually they can't make it themselves.

"I like to think I'm productive, that I put in a day's work. It's not as much as I used to, but I try.

"The old Indians, when they thought they couldn't contribute anymore, they knew enough to let nature take its course.

"So, I'm here. It's okay. Life is good. You don't have to go very far to find a guy worse off than you are. A lot of people are a lot worse, I'll tell you."

In private moments he had confided darker feelings to his sister. "I know there are days when Ted has told me he wished Rhoda had just let the whole thing go," Judy said one day a few months before her brother died. She was sipping iced tea in her tidy kitchen, with neatly arranged cookware and doilies on tabletops. On the walls were dozens of pictures of the family, including her little brother Ted.

Shortly before her brother died, Judy said, "He keeps asking me: 'What am I here for?' And I say, 'I don't know, Ted, but you're here, and after what you've been through, there must be a reason.'"

It was nearly spring, about five years after the fire, and the orchard was again calling to Ted, a finch yearning for his beloved branch. Twenty years earlier he had planted the orchard. On the south side of the old farmhouse, the grassy spot had two cherry trees, two pear trees, one peach, one plum, a cottonwood, a butternut, and a black walnut. There were several apple trees, which flowered with pinkish buds. There were two stately old ash trees, planted years earlier by Grandma Cora.

There were also birches, Norway pines, blue spruce, Austrian pines, an American chestnut, and oak trees. In the spring, when all the leaves filled in, the trees filled the whole ground with cool quiet shadows. Sitting at the house, Ted said, "There's nothing nicer than going down through there in the spring when the trees bloom and give off their scent."

INDEX

Ethics, *See* Medical Ethics
Extracell, 151

Farm, injuries, 135–136. *See also* Traumatic Injury
Surveillance of Farmers. *See* National Institute for Occupational Safety and Health. *See* Tractors
Farmer Creed, 171–172; and Prairie Farmer Creed, 97
Farmer Fred, safety mannequin, 141–142
Farming, 160, 163, 171, 179, 185, 202; and international markets, 166; mortality statistics, 135; occupational hazards, 135; as a shrinking profession in America, 161
Fibrosis, 58
Finch, 93, 202, 207
Fink, Arnold, 27, 100–101, 113, 148, 161
Fink, Carollyn, 148
Fink, Chris, 30, 35, 40, 68, 74, 89, 105, 108, 110–111, 113, 115, 117, 157, 166–167, 173, 183–185, 188–190, 194, 197, 199–200, 203
Fink, Cora, 28–29, 135, 148, 163; and eloping, 99, 179; farming in her dress, 101, 113; running a policeman off the road and avoiding a ticket, 101
Fink, Deanna, 74, 89, 105, 110, 113–115, 117, 167, 193, 195

Fink, Elmer, 97, 99–101; death of 134–135, 149, 161, 180
Fink, Faith, 28
Fink, Gerald, 100, 163
Fink, John M., 92–95
Fink, Judy, 7, 29, 35–37, 66, 69, 75, 100, 101, 105, 108, 171, 207; and visiting Ted in the hospital, 80–82, 85, 87
Fink, June, 28, 100, 113
Fink, Peter, 25, 33, 67, 75, 77, 86, 87, 11, 157, 191, 194, 203, 204
Fink, Rhoda, 5–6, 15–21, 27, 190–191, 193–195, 198; and bedside manicures and grooming, 66, 83; burn-support group, 36, 62, 69; childhood, 104; Christmas tree in burn unit, 35–36, 39; concerns about Ted's hands, 34, 37, 71, 78, 82; discussions with doctors 31, 33, 35, 41; doubts about her decision, 37, 39, 41, 72; eviction, 70; flower gardening, 182; lottery tickets, 71; on marriage, 204–205; reflecting on Ted's survival, 203–204; religion, 19–20, 34, 71, 203, 204–205; Ted's wedding ring, 39–40; work, 23–24
Fink, Samantha, 166, 173, 195; and first crawl, 186; reaching for her grandpa, 192–193
Fink, Ted Arthur, 6, 15, 16–41, 64–78, 148, 156–161,

A NOTE ON THE AUTHOR

Michael McCarthy was born in St. Louis and studied at St. Louis University. For twenty-one years he was a reporter and editor for the *Wall Street Journal*, whose editors nominated his story on the Fink family for the Pulitzer Prize in feature writing. Mr. McCarthy is now studying for a master's degree at DePaul University and teaches in the journalism department of Columbia College in Chicago. He is married with four children.